# MEDITERRANEAN DIET FOR BEGINNERS

*A complete guide with over 100 original and traditional recipes to lose weight and get back in shape naturally by eating tasty and healthy foods*

## ELENA WHEATLY

# INTRODUCTION

In today's society, so many people are out of shape and suffering from chronic disease and pain. With forecast obesity levels set to rise by up to 33% in the next two decades (Finkelstein et al., 2012), and depression affecting more than 350 million globally (Marcus et al., 2012), it's no surprise that those suffering are looking for alternative ways to heal themselves naturally. By following the lifestyle diet included in this book, you will be well on your way to reducing weight naturally and improving your overall health. While protecting your body and mind from future ailments, you will also be enhancing your lifestyle dramatically.

The Mediterranean diet is the most successful lifestyle in the world and is backed by irrefutable evidence. Research supports the Mediterranean diet as a way to live longer and age healthily while preventing cardiovascular disease (*Diet Review: Mediterranean Diet*, 2018).

Over the past 60 years, the Mediterranean diet has taken the world by storm, and for very good reason. The inspiration for the diet came from the simple eating practices and the excellent health of the Mediterraneans living in the region. According to The Nutrition Source (2018), "At that time, these countries displayed low rates of chronic disease and higher than average adult life expectancy despite having limited access to healthcare."

This nutritionally balanced diet focuses more on fresh plants and whole foods taken from traditional Mediterranean recipes that are eaten in a particular pattern rather than a classical "strict diet." Backed up by the findings from scientific research—which we will discuss further—this is far from a "fad diet" and should be seriously considered in its entirety. It is an eating pattern immediately available to you that promotes long-term good health and nutrition.

Once you adopt the straightforward principles of this antioxidant-rich diet, you will find it easy to apply to your daily life and more likely to work successfully when followed in the long term. Considering the health benefits and the famous palatability of the diet, you can be sure to enjoy this eating regimen. As you embark on this journey to learn about the Mediterranean diet, you should be feeling excited because real, positive results await you.

## HISTORY

The Mediterranean diet was formulated in the 1960s and is still popular today as a nutritionally healthy and sustainable cultural model. Looking back, studies conclude that (Nestle, 1995):

Mediterranean diets were based mainly on plant foods, contained small amounts of animal foods, used olive oil as the principal fat, used alcohol in moderation, and balanced energy intake with energy expenditure. Substantial research—in quantity and quality—supports the very great health benefits of such dietary patterns.

Further research concludes that (Helsing, 1995):

Health data for the Mediterranean region during the past few decades do point to distinctly lower rates of chronic diseases in the European part of the region compared with other developed countries in the world. Epidemiologists and nutritionists, together with food historians, chefs, and food loving enthusiasts should continue to explore, exploit, and enjoy the potential of Mediterranean diets for health and pleasure alike. Immediate efforts should be instituted to preserve the ancient and healthful dietary traditions within the Mediterranean region and to encourage greater consumption of plant foods in industrialized populations consistent with virtually all current dietary recommendations for health promotion and disease prevention.

In 2013, the United Nations Educational, Scientific, and Cultural Organization (UNESCO) inscribed Italy, Greece, Portugal, Morocco, Spain, Cyprus, and Croatia on the Representative List of the Intangible Cultural Heritage of Humanity for the Mediterranean diet.

More than just a diet, the precepts for the Mediterranean diet revolve around knowledge passed down, including traditional crop growing and harvesting skills, daily activities, craftsmanship, domestic animal care, fishing, conservation, processing, cooking, and sharing food.

Eating together is the basis of the community culture where participants can engage, socialize, communicate, and identify with each other in an inclusive atmosphere. Hospitality, creativity, and diversity are encouraged while being neighborly, mutually respectful, and welcoming forms an integral part of the Mediterranean's outlook on life. These beliefs play a major role in their continued robustness and longevity.

## ABOUT THE AUTHOR

Elena Wheatly has a degree in biology and works for a large company that distributes food products. Her passion for cooking allowed her to quickly become known as an expert in the field of healthy diets and wellness. Her dedication to the study of new recipes combined with her continuous research to deepen her knowledge in recipes from all over the world has allowed her to become known to fans even outside the national borders.

Elena loves to travel and often visits Europe, and in particular Italy, of which she loves the regional cuisine. Currently, in her spare time, Elena works on a project shared with fitness experts that aims to sensitize young people to take care of themselves, using food as a source of well-being and combining it with fitness tips and advice to maintain a perfect physical shape.

Other books by Elena Wheatly: *Intermittent Fasting For Women Over 50: A Complete Guide for Beginners to Weight Loss, Living a Healthier Life, And a Younger Looking Self.*

# CHAPTER 1

# BENEFITS OF THE MEDITERRANEAN DIET

## HEALTH BENEFITS

### LOWERED RISK OF CHRONIC DISEASE

An enormous amount of research into the Mediterranean diet has been undertaken over the years, and the results are strongly in favor of adopting its eating pattern globally. With the current trend leaning more toward western style food like takeout and highly processed, salted, and sugary foods—now more than ever—we should be mindful that eating more healthily in the future will have a positive effect on our overall health.

The scientific facts note that adhering to this diet will protect against the onset of chronic degenerative disorders (Sofi et al., 2010). Additionally, sticking closely to the Mediterranean diet eating plan fulfills daily nutrient intake levels far better than western diets (Dernini et al., 2016).

If you're looking for a long-term dietary program that will help with an existing condition, this is the place to check the health benefits. Following are 14 chronic illnesses with brief research, study, and clinical trial results substantiating the facts. In the Mediterranean alone, life expectancy has increased by 13% (Ferro-Luzzi and Branca, 1995).

That's an excellent reason to continue learning more about this highly recommended nutritional eating system.

Age-related macular degeneration:

- Lower risk of advancing to chronic macular degeneration (Merle et al., 2015).

Alzheimer's disease:

- Increased neuroimaging and cognitive phenotypes that, when altered, are associated with Alzheimer's disease (Karstens et al., 2019).
- Highly decreased risk of Alzheimer's disease and mortality (Martinez-Lacoba et al., 2018).

Breast cancer:

- Less chance of lower breast cancer in postmenopausal women. Very low evidence of breast cancer in the Mediterranean region (Trichopoulou et al., 2010).
- 7% reduced risk of breast cancer (Martinez-Lacoba et al., 2018).

Cardiovascular disease:

- Improves risk factors of cardiovascular disease with additional dairy foods over an eight-week period (Wade et al., 2018).
- Lowers risk of cardiovascular disease and total mortality in seniors by reinforcing the benefits of virgin olive oil and wine (De la Torre et al., 2017).
- Far better than the low-fat diet due to ectopic fat loss around the heart (Tsaban et al., 2017).
- Reduces the risk of sudden cardiac death in women (Guasch-Ferré et al., 2016).
- Lower all-cause mortality with cardiovascular disease sufferers (Lopez-Garcia et al., 2013).

- Reduced risk of cardiovascular disease (Gaskins et al., 2010).
- Better long-term outlook for people who have suffered an acute coronary event (Chrysohoou et al., 2010).
- Useful tool against cardiovascular disease that reduces inflammation (Mena et al., 2008).

Cancer:

- 13% reduction in risk of overall cancer mortality (Martinez-Lacoba et al., 2018).
- Reduced risk of stomach and intestine cancer (Ferro-Luzzi and Branca, 1995).
- 27% reduced risk of gastric cancer (Martinez-Lacoba et al., 2018).
- Colorectal cancer reduced by 17% (Martinez-Lacoba et al., 2018).
- Reduction in prostate cancer by 4% (Martinez-Lacoba et al., 2018).
- Liver cancer reduced by 42% (Martinez-Lacoba et al., 2018).
- Head and neck cancer risk lowered by 60% (Martinez-Lacoba et al., 2018).
- Reduced risk of lung cancer and down 25% in Italy (Ferro-Luzzi and Branca, 1995).
- Lower skin cancer risk in women; namely Basal Cell Carcinoma and Melanoma (Mahamat-Saleh et al., 2019).

Frailty syndrome:

- Reduced risk in women (Strujik et al., 2020).

Hypertension:

- Reduced systolic blood pressure (Jospe et al., 2019).
- The risk of high diastolic blood pressure reduced by 63% and high systolic blood pressure by 87% (Martinez-Lacoba et al., 2018).

Kidney stones:

- Lower risk of developing kidney stones (Rodriguez et al., 2020).

Multiple sclerosis:

- The Mediterranean diet protects those with multiple sclerosis due to a reduction in consumption of the disease-causing compounds increasing the risk. The effective inhibitive action of the olive oil and high prebiotic content lowers the risk of MS and aids in chronic fatigue (Moravejolahkami et al., 2020).

Obesity:

- Induced weight loss with physical activity (Muralidharan et al., 2021).
- Continual moderate weight loss substantially decreases ectopic fat surrounding the heart (Tsaban et al., 2017).
- Prevents weight gain and obesity development (Romaguera et al., 2010).
- Significantly reduces weight gain, and slows down age-related weight gain (Beunza et al., 2010).
- Meaningful improvement of sexual function for women with metabolic syndrome (Esposito et al., 2007).

Osteoporosis:

- Significantly reduced the bone loss rate at the femoral neck in osteoporosis sufferers (Jennings et al., 2018).

Rheumatoid arthritis:

- By combining the Mediterranean diet with a dynamic exercise program, arthritic patients can improve their quality of life in conjunction with anti-rheumatoid medication (García-Morales et al., 2020).

Stroke:

- May alleviate the metabolite profiles that cause strokes (Guasch-Ferré et al., 2016).
- Decreased risk of stroke incidence (Gardener et al., 2011).
- Reduced risk of stroke is continually associated with adherence to the Mediterranean diet (Martinez-Lacoba et al., 2018).

Type 2 diabetes:

- Reduced glycated hemoglobin (Jospe et al., 2019).
- The Mediterranean diet could counteract the detrimental effects of glycolysis/gluconeogenesis-related metabolites (Guasch-Ferré et al., 2020).
- Improves remnant cholesterol levels in people with type 2 diabetes (Gomez-Marin et al., 2018).
- Long-term consumption of the Mediterranean diet rich in olive oil improves postprandial lipemia concentrations associated with cardiovascular disease mainly in people with type 2 diabetes (Gomez-Marin et al., 2018).
- Lower risk of frailty syndrome in older female diabetes sufferers (Lopez-Garcia et al., 2018).

## ALLEVIATION OF MENTAL HEALTH ISSUES

One of the most common forms of mental health illness is dementia, with more than 50 million people suffering globally. A total of 65% of cases are classed as Alzheimer's disease. Dementia is a major cause of dependency and disability among the elderly population and has a social, economic, and psychological impact on sufferers and their carers (World Health Organisation, 2020).

Studies show that meaningful improvements in mental health can be attained by choosing to eat in the Mediterranean pattern (Parletta et al., 2017). Research into the Mediterranean diet as a way to reduce the risk and improve cognition has brought positive results to mental health issues, some of which are listed below.

Cognitive impairment:

- 7-16% lower risk of later-life cognitive impairment in Chinese adults (Wu et al., 2019).
- Continually higher cognitive capacity in older people over an 11-year period with nuts, legumes, and whole grains playing an integral part (Wengreen et al., 2013).
- Improved cognitive function and reduced risk of poor cognition (Shannon et al., 2019).
- Significantly reduced risk of all-cause dementia (Martinez-Lacoba et al., 2018).

Depression:

- Hinders depressive disorders (Sánchez-Villegas et al., 2009).
- Lowers the risk of depression and improves the symptoms of severe depression and remission rates (Ventriglio et al., 2020).
- Enjoying the process of preparing, cooking, and eating wholesome Mediterranean diet food in groups can prevent depression (Parletta et al., 2017).
- Best results for effectively diminishing depressive symptoms (Fond et al., 2020).
- The Mediterranean diet paired with aerobic exercise leads to similar effects of antidepressants used in clinical depression treatment (Bremner et al., 2020).


IMPROVED LIFESTYLE

Changing your eating habits to that of the Mediterranean-style diet can definitely lead to an improved lifestyle. Following are some results you can expect:

- Enjoy a better health-related quality of life with mental clarity due to the antioxidant levels of the food (Bonaccio et al., 2013).
- Significantly improves the psychological and emotional well-being and happiness of adolescents (López-Olivares et al., 2020).
- The Mediterranean diet's sustainable eating pattern contributes to a healthy life and provides food security for future generations (Martinez-Lacoba et al., 2018).
- Increased self-esteem and feeling of wellness (Bremner et al., 2020).
- Higher rates of self-perceived physical and mental health functionality are directly connected to using the Mediterranean diet long-term (Muñoz et al., 2008).
- Experience more vitality and increased optimism with improvement in healthy behavior and enhanced positive thinking (Echeverría et al., 2020).
- Enjoy increasing social benefits by sharing more leisurely meals with family and friends in an inclusive atmosphere.
- Spending time in the sun during outdoor activities increases vitamin D generation which helps to keep muscles, bones, and teeth healthy.
- Knowingly participate in an environmentally sustainable diet.

## ENVIRONMENTAL BENEFITS

The Mediterranean diet is sustainable with a lower environmental impact compared to other diets. Generating lower greenhouse gases, a smaller water footprint, energy consumption, and land use, the diet is mainly plant-based with fewer animal-based products included. The footprint of the food environment and natural resources are markedly reduced while conserving the biodiversity of the region (Dernini et al., 2016).

By reducing the intake of animal-based products to just twice a week, the environmental impact produced by consuming food can be effectively lowered by up to one-third (Ruini et al., 2015).

The transport carbon footprint can be dramatically reduced by using homegrown and foods produced locally (Echeverría et al., 2020).

## PERSONAL BENEFITS

By now you have a better understanding of just how beneficial the Mediterranean diet is. Following is a list of the personal benefits you can expect when using this eating pattern in conjunction with daily exercise and shared meals:

- Prevention of chronic disease
- Natural weight loss
- Clearer thinking and improved reaction times
- Overall better health
- Improved skin and hair condition
- Fewer mood swings
- A positive outlook
- More enjoyment at mealtimes
- More engaging social gatherings
- Healthy aging
- Increased lifespan
- Improved immunity and respiratory fitness

# CHAPTER 2
# MEDITERRANEAN DIET FOOD
## BASIC FOOD GROUPS

This diet is based on fresh, healthy food originating in the Mediterranean region, including plant-based foods and oily fish high in omega-3. Low amounts of red meat and processed meats are consumed weekly as well as red wine. Drink plenty of water every day and exercise regularly. This eating pattern easily adapts to the food available in your region.

### *High Intake Food Eaten Daily*

You can enjoy fruit, vegetables, olive oil, nuts, seeds, legumes, whole grains, and dairy every day.

### *Medium Intake Food Eaten in Moderation*

Fish, seafood, legumes, white meat, and red wine can be consumed several times a week.

### *Low Intake Food to Limit*

Eat less red meat, processed meat, and homemade desserts.

### *Food to Avoid*

- Keep red meat to a minimum.

- Added sugar products like sodas, candy, store-bought baked goods, and artificial juices.
- Processed delicatessen meats like bacon, sausage, salami, and hot dogs.
- Stay away from hard liquor and only drink one or two glasses of red wine at most per day.
- Choose healthier whole grain options rather than refined grains like white rice and white flour products like white bread, white pasta, and white pizza dough.
- Butter and animal fats should be replaced with a trickle of olive oil.
- Avoid hydrogenated oils like canola oil, palm oil, and soybean oil.

## *The Mediterranean Diet Pyramid*

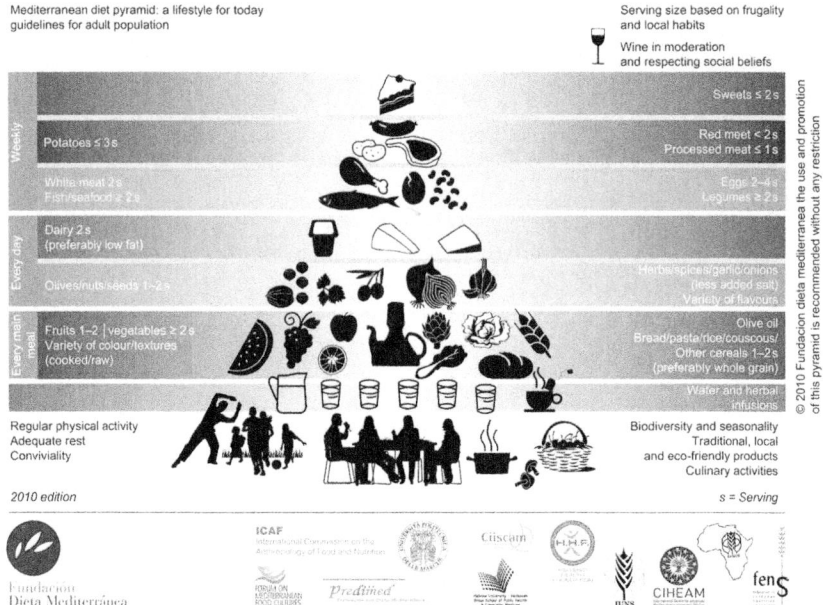

## FOOD SUBSTITUTIONS

There are some disorders and food eating preferences that we can make considerations for with the Mediterranean diet.

### *Coeliac*

Coeliacs suffer from gluten intolerance and will find that most of the food in the Mediterranean diet is acceptable, especially considering that it supplements the nutrients that may be lacking from a regular gluten-free diet. This diet is made up of simple dishes that coeliacs will enjoy and benefit from.

Most coeliacs will be used to looking for products that are free from gluten—as more new gluten-free products are being produced and offered today—and now they should also look for whole grain alternatives.

Following is a list of suggestions for substituting recipe ingredients in this book:

- Cook polenta made from whole grain cornmeal.
- Choose whole grain gluten-free crackers and bread.
- Use quinoa to replace bulgur wheat in dishes like tabbouleh.
- Buy gluten-free whole grain pasta like buckwheat or wholemeal varieties.
- Use brown rice or gluten-free steel-cut oats for risotto.
- Lentils can be substituted for rice.
- Use gluten-free panko breadcrumbs instead of regular breadcrumbs.
- Hummus works well as a replacement for mayonnaise as a dip, on pizzas, or with crackers.
- Add chopped nuts to roasted vegetables or pasta dishes to add texture.

### *Vegan*

Vegans don't eat foods that come from animals, and the Mediterranean diet is well suited to this philosophy as it is full of nourishing plant-based foods. Following are some suggested substitutions that can be made to the recipe ingredients in this book:

- Use plant-based protein in place of seafood, meat, and poultry. These products include healthful anti-inflammatory properties.
- Choose tofu, tempeh, and beans in small portions as another replacement for protein.
- Use nuts and seeds like walnuts, chia seeds, flaxseeds, and hemp seeds as a replacement for seafood as they are high in omega-3 and protein.

### *Vegetarian*

Depending on the type of vegetarian you are, lacto-ovo or vegetarian, you can substitute the same ingredients mentioned in the vegan section for proteins that you don't eat. Almost everything else on this diet will agree with your preferred food choices.

## FOOD RECOMMENDATIONS

You will find that the food choices in this eating regimen are full of delicious produce. Adult serving sizes are frugal as they can be filling, and there is no wastage of food. Leftovers can be smartly incorporated into meals the following day.

For simplicity and practicality, the following food lists have been updated to include a wider variety of readily available items. Of course, if you have trouble sourcing any of the food listed in this book, you can always substitute, or consider growing the required plants. Frequenting your local market takes advantage of seasonal produce, and always ensure produce is washed gently but thoroughly at home.

### *Vegetables*

The foundation of the Mediterranean diet includes building meals around fresh vegetables, and you can eat them in abundance. Mediterraneans often make use of edible weeds as green additions to their soups and stews.

Vegetables: Two or more servings per day:

- artichokes
- arugula (rocket)
- asparagus
- beans
- beetroot
- bell peppers
- broad beans
- broccoli
- broccolini
- brussels sprouts
- bok choy

- butter beans (lima)
- cabbage
- caperberries
- capers
- capsicum
- carrots
- cauliflower
- celeriac
- celery
- chicory (witloof)
- chokos
- choy sum
- collards
- cucumbers
- dandelion greens
- eggplant (aubergine)
- edamame
- endive
- fennel
- garlic
- kale (Cavallo Nero)
- leeks
- lettuces
- mushrooms
- mustard greens
- nettles
- okra
- onions
- parsnip
- peas
- peppers
- potatoes (3 or fewer serves per week)
- pumpkin
- purslane
- radishes
- rutabaga (swede)

- shallots
- silverbeet
- snow peas
- sow thistle (puha)
- spinach
- spring onions (scallions)
- swede
- sweet potatoes
- tomatoes
- turnips
- watercress
- zucchinis (courgette)
- yams

## *Fruit*

The Mediterranean diet recommends eating fruit after the main meal, but it can also be eaten at breakfast time. This is where you will get a sugar fix in the future.

Fruit: One to two servings daily (one preferably after the main meal):

- acai berry
- apples
- apricots
- avocados
- bananas
- blackberries
- blackcurrant
- blueberries
- boysenberries
- capers
- cherries
- clementines
- coconut
- cranberries
- currants

- custard apple
- dates (preferably medjool for higher fiber)
- dragon fruit (strawberry pear)
- elderberries
- feijoa
- figs
- gooseberries
- grapefruit
- grapes
- guavas
- kiwifruit
- kumquat
- lemons
- lime
- loquats
- lychees
- mangoes
- mangosteen
- melons (honeydew, rockmelon (cantaloupe), watermelon)
- mulberries
- nectarines
- olives
- oranges
- papaya (pawpaw)
- passionfruit
- peaches
- pears
- persimmon
- pineapple
- plums
- pomegranates
- prunes
- pummelo
- quince
- raisins
- raspberries

- rhubarb
- strawberries
- tangerines (mandarins)
- tamarillo (tree tomato)

### Increased Omega-3 Fatty Acids

Omega-3 is a well-known contributor to overall good health containing high-quality protein, vitamins, and nutrients. There are several food groups that contain omega-3 in the Mediterranean diet listed below. Canned seafood and smoked fish are acceptable.

Fish/Seafood: Two or more servings a week (preferably cold water types high in omega-3):

- abalone
- anchovies
- Atlantic mackerel
- bluefish
- caviar
- cockles
- clams (vongole)
- crab
- eel
- herring
- lake whitefish
- lobster
- mussels
- octopus
- oysters
- sablefish (black cod)
- salmon
- sardines
- scallops
- sea bass
- shrimp (prawns)
- squid

- striped bass
- sturgeon
- tilapia
- trout
- tuna (albacore)
- whelk
- yellowtail

Olives, Nuts, and Seeds - One to two servings a day (choose unsalted nuts):

- almonds
- brazil nuts
- cashews
- chestnuts
- chia seeds
- fennel seeds
- flaxseed
- hazelnuts
- hemp seeds
- macadamias
- olives (all types)
- pecans
- pine nuts
- pistachios
- pumpkin seeds
- sesame seeds
- sunflower seeds
- tempeh
- walnuts

### *Olive Oil*

One of the most beneficial food groups in the Mediterranean diet is olive oil rich in omega-9 and antioxidants. It can be used in cooking, sprinkled over food and salad, or used for preserving food. We've included vinegar here too, as it has healthful properties.

Olive oil: Use liberally up to 50 mls per day (2–4 tbsp):

- extra virgin avocado oil
- canola oil
- extra virgin olive oil (recommended as it is less refined with a higher concentration of antioxidants)
- flaxseed oil
- grapeseed oil
- olive oil
- peanut oil
- safflower oil

Vinegar: Use with oil to make salad dressings adding herbs and spices for variety:

- apple cider vinegar
- balsamic vinegar
- champagne vinegar
- fig vinegar
- red wine vinegar
- white wine vinegar

### Dairy Products

Eaten in moderation, the following dairy products add flavor to meals while providing calcium, proteins, and nutrients. Milk isn't part of the Mediterranean diet; however, you can use unsweetened soy or almond milk in small quantities, as legumes and nuts are elements of the diet. Avoid processed cheeses that are high in fat and sodium.

Eggs: Two to four eggs per week (preferably free range):

- chicken eggs
- duck eggs
- quail eggs

Dairy: Two servings a day (preferably low fat):

- blue cheese
- bocconcini
- brie cheese
- burrata
- chevre cheese
- corvo cheese (aged cheddar)
- cottage cheese
- cream (low fat)
- feta cheese
- goats cheese
- Greek yogurt
- halloumi cheese
- kashkaval
- labneh made from Greek yogurt
- manchego cheese
- mascarpone
- mozzarella cheese
- parmigiano-reggiano cheese (parmesan)
- pecorino cheese
- ricotta cheese
- swiss cheese
- tofu

## *Legumes*

While legumes are a good substitute for meat, they have other wonderful properties such as no cholesterol, low in fat, and high in minerals, beneficial fats, and fiber. Always rinse canned legumes with fresh water to reduce the sodium content.

Legumes: Two or more servings a week:

- black beans
- black-eyed peas
- borlotti beans
- cannellini beans (white kidney bean)
- chickpeas (garbanzo beans)

- fava beans
- haricots (navy bean, pearl haricot, white pea bean, pea bean)
- kidney beans
- lentils
- mung beans
- peanuts
- pinto beans
- soybeans
- split peas

## Whole Grains

Subtracting processed food from your diet is a positive step toward good health. Eating unrefined whole grains quickly fills the stomach due to the high fiber content. Use whole grain or wholemeal flour while avoiding refined white flour.

Whole grains: One to two servings per day:

- almond meal
- barley
- bread (preferably whole grain or wholemeal)
- brown rice
- buckwheat
- bulgur
- ciabatta
- corn
- cornmeal
- couscous
- durum
- farro
- focaccia
- freekeh
- lavash
- millet
- pasta (preferably whole grain, whole wheat, buckwheat, or wholemeal)

- pita bread
- polenta (corn grits)
- popcorn
- quinoa
- rice
- rye
- sorghum
- sprouted bread
- whole oats
- whole wheat

## Meat

Traditionally, Mediterraneans don't often eat meat—compared to industrialized countries—and most of their animals are grass fed with free-ranging poultry. Think of serving meat the opposite way that you do now. Eat it less often as a side dish instead of incorporating the dish around the meat. Considering it as more of a garnish over vegetables or a soup or stew addition makes it easier to adapt and enjoy in this diet.

Poultry: Two servings per week (trimmed of fat):

- chicken
- duck
- guinea fowl
- quail
- turkey

Red meat: Two or fewer servings per week (lean cuts or trim the fat):

- beef
- goat
- lamb
- mutton
- pork

## Herbs and Spices

A delicious addition to any dish, herbs and spices will add an abundance of flavor to meals. Rich in phytochemicals, they help reduce cell damage and ward off inflammation.

Herbs and spices: No limit:

- allspice
- anise
- basil
- bay leaves
- bergamot
- borage
- caraway
- cardamom
- cassia
- cayenne pepper
- celery seed
- chervil
- chilies
- chives
- cinnamon
- cloves
- coriander
- cumin
- curry leaf
- dill
- fennel
- fenugreek
- garlic
- ginger
- horseradish
- lavender
- lemon balm
- lemongrass
- lemon verbena
- licorice
- lovage

- mac
- marjoram
- mint
- mustard
- nepitella (mentuccia)
- nutmeg
- oregano
- paprika
- parsley
- pepper
- peppermint
- poppy seed
- rosemary
- rue
- saffron
- sage
- sorrel
- star anise
- spearmint
- sumac
- tarragon
- thyme
- turmeric
- vanilla

### Red Wine

Red grape skins contain resveratrol, which may slow down the aging process and lower blood sugar levels. In the Mediterranean diet, red wine is consumed in moderation, usually with the main meal which is often at lunchtime. If you don't drink wine, then leave it out or consider replacing it with unsweetened purple grape juice.

Red wine: One glass a day for women and up to two glasses a day for men.

Tea and coffee can be consumed in moderation without sugar.

### *Avoid Sugar Cravings*

It's best to stay away from sugary processed foods and to enjoy sweet, fresh fruit instead. Mediterraneans usually only eat honey with cakes on special occasions. Homemade treats can be eaten infrequently as long as they are cooked with the Mediterranean principles in mind.

Sweets: Two or fewer servings per week:

- biscotti
- dark chocolate
- fruit high in antioxidants and vitamins like blackberries, raspberries, oranges, and grapefruit
- gelato
- mousse
- olive oil cake
- olive oil muffins
- sorbet
- treats made with nuts, fruit, whole grains, and little sugar content

# CHAPTER 3
# HOW TO ADOPT THE MEDITERRANEAN DIET
## LIFESTYLE

The Mediterranean lifestyle is one that you will come to enjoy as you put thought into the food you eat, take care in meal preparation, share meals together in a convivial atmosphere, and maintain a healthy disposition and outlook. It is important to exercise daily, even if it's just a walk in the sunshine, and to get at least the minimum amount of sleep for your age each night.

The Mediterranean diet is not a strict calorie-counting diet but a way of life that will improve your overall health, mentally and physically. It's effortless to make the transition, whether you decide to undertake the principles gradually or embrace them completely. Either way, you can be assured of taking a positive step toward living a healthy lifestyle using one of the most successful, evidence-backed eating regimes in the world.

## ONE MEAL AT A TIME

A 4-week meal plan is included at the end of this book to get you started quickly. There are many meals you can choose to eat in the order you prefer—according to the ingredients you currently have on hand—or you may choose to select one meal at a time.

At first, it makes sense to take this lifestyle one meal at a time to become successful in following the principles. Don't feel overwhelmed by the enormity of the Mediterranean diet. Instead, ensure you keep it simple to make it easier to follow.

## ONE DAY AT A TIME

If you lead a busy life and feel that it's too much of a distinct change in your dietary habits, consider taking this new lifestyle one day at a time. At the end of each day, congratulate yourself for continuing the journey with good intentions, then start the following day with a positive outlook. You'll feel much more optimistic!

## COOK YOUR MEALS

Plan your meals ahead of time and cook them yourself. If you are busy with a family, you can solicit help from your partner and children to build inclusiveness and enjoy the experience together. Discuss good things about your day as you prepare meals together.

Get help setting the table to look inviting and consider inviting a friend or neighbor to join you. After all, the Mediterranean lifestyle includes social interaction and hospitality.

Ensure you read the recipes you will be cooking in advance so you can be sure of the necessary steps to take. Make sure you have all the ingredients ready at hand to make the cooking process quick and easy. Tidy up as you go to make cleaning less of a chore afterward.

If you don't consider yourself to be a "good cook," that's fine. You don't have to be a good cook to make the simple yet tasty recipes in this book. They say, "Practice makes perfect," and you will find that your skills improve over time with experience. You may also discover that you can create your own recipes with ingredients you love to eat. We all remember our favorites.

Most important of all, keep calm and cook with love, then the food will shine.

## TIPS FOR DINING OUT

Dining out needn't be a problem when you follow the Mediterranean diet. Simply look for meals that are either vegetarian or have little meat included. Choosing soup, salad, and vegetable-based food is a smart way to eat out.

If it's a special occasion and you still feel hungry, consider a small dessert or cheese and fruit plate as a reward for sticking to the diet, then share it.

There are many beautiful recipes in this book that can be made for healthy and rewarding entertainment by doubling the recipe. There are also some great recipes in the appetizers section that can be used for party finger food.

## TIPS FOR PARENTS

When you lead a busy life balancing home, work, and family commitments, it can seem like there aren't enough hours in the day to do everything that needs to be done. However, if you plan ahead and know what you will be cooking for dinner, you can consider this in the morning by taking out any frozen ingredients that need thawing and leave them in the fridge to thaw during the day. Additionally, you can pull out vegetables and other ingredients that you will need in advance, then place them in a convenient location in the fridge or on the kitchen bench to be close at hand later.

Here are some further tips to consider:

- Stick to the principles of the Mediterranean diet when preparing school lunches by including salads, veggie sticks, fresh fruit, nuts, and cheese.
- Avoid waste by using leftovers in lunches to take to work and reheat.
- There is no hard and fast rule that states you have to undertake the cooking of meals alone. Ask for help in the kitchen or dining room when you need it and show gratitude.

- Teach your children about the nutritional facts and benefits of the food they are eating, encourage them to eat healthy food, and feel good about it.
- When you have time on your hands and you feel like cooking, consider preparing a double-sized meal, then freeze the unused half to use another day.
- Some children are fussy about eating vegetables, and the best way to get them to enjoy eating them is to serve them up looking delicious and inviting rather than plain and boring. Consider drizzling a little olive oil over veggies then sprinkling with nuts, seeds, and fragrant fresh herbs.
- Try using smaller cuts of veggies in soups and casseroles, and include legumes like chickpeas, lentils, or cannellini beans to add tasty yet filling nutrients.
- Use veggie sticks with dips scattered with nuts to add texture and flavor.
- Adding sweeter vegetables like roasted beetroot and sweet potato with the more bland vegetables like potatoes can make them more interesting and tasty to eat—especially when you crumble feta over the top.
- Use a colorful variety of vegetables and garnish with sliced poultry or meat to create a nourishing meal.

# CHAPTER 4
# SNACK RECIPES

## SNACKS

- Where possible, most of the measurements in these recipes have been calculated for 1 | 2 | 4 servings.
- Nutrition calculations for fruit and vegetable sizes have been set to medium.
- Cook time is calculated by prep time plus cook time plus anything else done in between.

## CRUNCHY MEDITERRANEAN BITES

This is a quick and easy snack or great for finger food at a party. Great on their own or with dipping sauce or tzatziki.

**Time:** 35 minutes

**Serving Size:** 1 | 2 | 4 servings

**Prep Time:** 20 minutes

**Cook Time:** 15 minutes

**Nutritional Facts/Info:**

Calories 267

Carbs 16.5 g

Fat 16.9 g

Protein 14.8 g

**Ingredients:**

- ½ | 1 | 2 cups plain wholemeal flour
- ½ | 1 | 2 tsp baking powder
- 1 egg (whisked)
- 30 | 60 | 120 g feta (crumbled)
- 2 tbsp | ¼ | ½ cup mixed pitted olives (chopped)
- 1 | 2 | 4 tomatoes (quartered, deseeded, and finely chopped)
- ⅛ | ¼ | ½ cup basil leaves (chopped)
- Extra virgin olive oil for deep frying
- Mixed chopped herbs

**Directions:**

1. Pour oil into a large saucepan or wok until it comes a quarter up the side. Heat on medium-high until temperature reaches 320 °F/160 °C on a thermometer (or when a wooden spoon end standing in the oil bubbles).
2. In a bowl, mix the flour, baking powder, and a pinch of salt together.
3. Spoon a well in the center of the flour, then add the egg and 2 tbsp water. Mix together until it becomes a stiff batter.
4. Add the feta, olives, tomato, and basil, then stir to combine.
5. Using a tablespoon, add spoonfuls of mixture to the hot oil for a few minutes.
6. When golden underneath, carefully flip over and continue to cook for 3 minutes or until completely cooked.
7. Remove from pan onto a paper towel. Repeat steps 5 and 6 with remaining mixture.

8. Sprinkle with the mixed herbs and serve.

## FRUITY POPCORN BARS

Children will enjoy helping to make these healthy, low-fat alternatives to muesli bars that are lovely to eat.

**Time:** 15 minutes

**Serving Size:** Makes 24

**Prep Time:** 15 minutes

**Nutritional Facts/Info:**

Calories 85

Carbs 11.1 g

Fat 4.5 g

Protein 1.8 g

**Ingredients:**

- 4 cups plain unsalted popcorn
- ¾ cup dried figs
- ½ cup dried cranberries
- ½ cup roasted almonds
- ½ cup desiccated coconut
- 1 cup tahini
- 1 tbsp pure honey

**Directions:**

1. Line a 12 x 5 in/30 x 15 cm slice pan with parchment paper.
2. Add popcorn to a food processor and pulse until roughly chopped. Remove to a mixing bowl.
3. Add figs, cranberries, and almonds to the processor, then pulse until finely chopped. Transfer to mixing bowl.

4. Add the remaining ingredients and stir to combine.
5. Spoon mixture into slice pan and smooth out evenly. Chill.
6. Cut mixture into 24 pieces and store in an airtight container. Enjoy.

## SPICY ZUCCHINI AND PARSNIP CHIPS

These delightful crispy chips are a healthy gluten-free alternative to whole grain crackers that can be stored in ziplock bags for up to 2 weeks. Try them with any dip like hummus or store-bought low-fat dips. If you have a food processor with a cutting disc or a mandolin to use, it could save preparation time.

**Time:** 2 hours 40 minutes

**Serving Size:** 1 | 2 | 4 servings

**Prep Time:** 40 minutes

**Cook Time:** 1½ hours

**Nutritional Facts/Info:**

Calories 100

Carbs 16.1 g

Fat 4.1 g

Protein 2.2 g

**Ingredients:**

- ½ | 1 | 2 large zucchinis (washed, ends cut, and sliced into ⅛ in/3 cm rounds)
- ½ | 1 | 2 large parsnips (washed, ends cut, and sliced into ⅛ in/3 cm rounds)
- Salt to cover
- Extra virgin olive oil
- ½ tsp chili powder
- ½ tsp smoky paprika

- ½ tsp ground coriander
- ½ tsp garlic salt
- ½ tsp ground fennel seeds

## Directions:

1. Set oven to 240 °F/120 °C and line a large oven tray with parchment paper.
2. Mix the spices together in a small bowl, then set aside with the sliced parsnip.
3. Lay paper towels on a bench, then place the zucchini slices onto the paper. Sprinkle with salt.
4. Cover the zucchinis with another layer of paper towel, then place a heavy baking dish or chopping board over the zucchinis to weigh down squeezing out excess juice. Leave for 20 minutes.
5. Brush or spray the parchment paper in the tray with extra virgin olive oil.
6. Remove the top layer of paper towel from the zucchini, then distribute the zucchini and parsnip rounds in a single layer on the tray. Brush or spray lightly with oil.
7. Dust the vegetable slices with the spice mix.
8. Slow cook in the oven for 1½ hours until crispy, checking occasionally.
9. Test for crispiness and if some aren't crisp enough, remove the crispy chips and return the others to cook a little longer.
10. Arrange on a plate and serve on their own or with a dip. Enjoy.

MAPLE SEED BALLS

Great to pop in your mouth when peckish and healthy for lunch boxes with 70 calories per ball.

**Time:** 20 minutes

**Serving Size:** 1 | 2 | 4 servings (makes 15)

**Prep Time:** 20 minutes

**Nutritional Facts/Info:**

Calories 264

Carbs 23.7 g

Fat 17.1 g

Protein 7.3 g

**Ingredients:**

- 2 tbsp | ¼ | ½ cup sunflower seeds
- 2 tbsp | ¼ | ½ cup pepita seeds
- 2 tbsp | ¼ | ½ cup whole grain rolled oats
- ½ | 1 | 2 tsp flaxseeds
- ½ | 1 | 2 tsp hemp seeds
- ½ | 1 | 2 tbsp tahini
- ¾ | 1¼ | 2½ tbsp maple syrup
- ½ | 1 | 2 tbsp sesame seeds (toasted)

**Directions:**

1. In a food processor or blender, add sunflower seeds, pepitas, and oats, then blend until finely chopped.
2. Transfer to a large bowl and add flaxseed, hemp seeds, 1 tbsp water, and a pinch of salt. Stir to combine.
3. Add tahini and maple syrup then stir to combine.
4. In a small bowl, add the toasted sesame seeds.
5. Roll level tablespoon mixture into balls then in sesame seeds to coat. Place on a plate.
6. Continue with remaining mixture and sesame seeds. Enjoy.

CRUDITES WITH HERBED NUTTY DIP

Always scrumptious and satisfying to eat, this veggie dip can be made into a large plate to share or mini servings to suit.

**Time:** 15 minutes

**Serving Size:** 1 | 2 | 4 servings

**Prep Time:** 15 minutes

**Nutritional Facts/Info:**

Calories 88

Carbs 15.7 g

Fat 2.2 g

Protein 2.9 g

**Ingredients:**

- 2 tbsp | ¼ | ½ cup hummus
- ¼ | ½ | 1 tbsp low-fat Greek yogurt
- 1 tbsp | 2 tbsp | ¼ cup chopped hazelnuts
- 2 tbsp | ¼ | ½ tbsp parsley (chopped)
- ¼ | ½ | 1 tsp fresh basil (chopped)
- ¼ | ½ | 1 tsp fresh rosemary (chopped)
- ¼ | ½ | 1 apple (cored, sliced)
- ⅛ | ¼ | ½ medium carrot (peeled, sliced into batons)
- ⅛ | ¼ | ½ medium cucumber (peeled, sliced into batons)
- ⅛ | ¼ | ½ medium capsicum (deseeded, sliced into batons)
- ⅛ | ¼ | ½ medium celery (sliced into batons)
- 2 tbsp | ¼ | ½ cup pitted olives
- ¼ | ½ | 1 tomato (cut into small wedges)
- 12 | 25 | 50 g light cheddar or tasty cheese (sliced into batons)

**Directions:**

1. In a small bowl, mix the hummus, yogurt, and hazelnuts together.
2. Sprinkle with the herbs.
3. Arrange the fruit and veggies around the dip bowl and serve.

PEPITA DATE MUFFINS

A tasty little snack to fill the gap between meals.

**Time:** 50 minutes

**Serving Size:** Makes 12 muffins

**Prep Time:** 10 minutes

**Cook Time:** 30 minutes

**Nutritional Facts/Info:**

Calories 135

Carbs 19.1 g

Fat 5.1 g

Protein 4.7 g

**Ingredients:**

- 1 tsp mixed spice (coriander, ginger, nutmeg, cassia, and cloves)
- ½ cup extra virgin olive oil
- 200 g dates (pitted, chopped)
- 1 orange (juiced, zested)
- 2 tbsp golden syrup
- ½ cup LSA (mixed linseeds, sunflower seeds, and almonds)
- 250 g low-fat Greek yogurt
- 2 cups wholemeal self-raising flour
- 2 free-range eggs (whisked)
- ½ cup pepita seeds

**Directions:**

1. Set oven to 400 °F/200 °C. Line a 12-hole muffin pan with paper cases or spray a 24 mini-muffin tray with extra virgin olive oil spray.
2. In a small saucepan over medium heat, add the dates, olive oil,

½ cup of water, golden syrup, orange rind, and ½ cup of orange juice. Cook, stirring until hot, then remove from heat to cool.

3. Combine flour, LSA, and mixed spice in a large bowl.
4. Whisk eggs and yogurt together until smooth. Blend into the flour.
5. Blend the cooled date liquid into the flour until just combined.
6. Spoon into paper cases and sprinkle with pepitas.
7. Cook for 20-25 minutes until golden. Enjoy.

## ROASTED CHICKPEA SNACK

A crunchy, addictive snack best eaten on the day it's made. Any favorite spices can be added to this recipe, and they're a great addition to salads.

**Time:** 50 minutes

**Serving Size:** 1 | 2 | 4 servings

**Prep Time:** 10 minutes

**Cook Time:** 35 minutes

**Nutritional Facts/Info:**

Calories 129

Carbs 11.2 g

Fat 7.7 g

Protein 3.6 g

**Ingredients:**

- 100 | 200 | 400 g can chickpeas or garbanzos (rinsed, drained)
- ½ | 1 | 2 tbsp extra virgin olive oil
- ¼ | ½ | 1 tsp ground rosemary
- ¼ | ½ | 1 tbsp lemon zest
- 1 pinch |2 pinches | ¼ tsp ground cumin
- 1 pinch |2 pinches | ¼ tsp paprika

- 1 pinch |2 pinches | ¼ tsp ground coriander
- 1 pinch |2 pinches | ¼ tsp garlic powder

**Directions:**

1. Set oven to 375 °F/190 °C and line a baking tray with parchment paper.
2. Spread the chickpeas out on paper towel, cover, and pat to dry.
3. Tip the chickpeas into a bowl with the oil and season. Toss to cover.
4. Tip chickpeas onto baking tray and spread out evenly.
5. Roast for 25–35 minutes or until crispy and golden, shaking the pan occasionally.
6. Mix the herbs and spices together then set aside.
7. Remove from oven and sprinkle with the mixed herbs and spices.
8. Toss and serve.

SUMMER MELON SNACK

This no-cholesterol dish is a lovely indulgence on a hot day while being healthy and nutritious.

**Time:** 15 minutes

**Serving Size:** 1 | 2 | 4 servings

**Prep Time: 15 minutes**

**Nutritional Facts/Info:**

Calories 108

Carbs 16.6 g

Fat 3.4 g

Protein 2.5 g

**Ingredients:**

- 75 | 150 | 300 g honeydew melon (peeled)
- 75 | 150 | 300 g rockmelon (cantaloupe, peeled)
- 50 | 100 | 200 g black grapes (picked)
- 1 tbsp | 2 tbsp| ¼ cup seed and nut mix
- ⅛ | ¼ | ½ tsp minced ginger
- ⅛ | ¼ | ½ tbsp lime juice
- Balsamic glaze (to drizzle)
- 2 tbsp | ¼ | ½ cup fresh basil leaves (picked, to serve)

**Directions:**

1. Using a melon baller, scoop balls out of the melons into a bowl.
2. Add the grapes, seed and nut mix, ginger, and lime juice, then gently mix together.
3. Drizzle lightly with balsamic glaze.
4. Sprinkle with basil.
5. Serve chilled.


SPANISH SARDINE SALAD ON TOAST

Eaten on toasted wholemeal, this is a healthy, wholesome snack for any family member.

**Time:** 15 minutes

**Serving Size:** 1 | 2 | 4 servings

**Prep Time:** 5 minutes

**Cook Time:** 5 minutes

**Nutritional Facts/Info:**

Calories 323

Carbs 19 g

Fat 21.2 g

Protein 15.3 g

**Ingredients:**

- ½ | 1 | 2 cans skinless and boneless Spanish style sardines (drained, oil reserved)
- 50 | 100 | 200 g mixed salad leaves
- 15 | 30 | 60 g prepared piquillo or roasted red peppers
- 15 | 30 | 60 g Spanish olives (sliced)
- ¼ | ½ | 1 small red onion (sliced finely)
- 15 | 30 | 60 g shaved manchego cheese
- 15 | 30 | 60 g slivered almonds
- 1 | 2 | 4 slices whole grain bread (toasted)

Dressing:

- ¾ |1½ | 3 tbsp fresh lemon juice
- ¼ | ¼ | 1 tsp lemon zest
- ¼ | ½ | reserved oil from sardines

**Directions:**

1. Break the sardines into bite-size pieces.
2. Mix dressing ingredients until combined, then toss with fish

and salad ingredients. Season.

3. Top salad with the manchego and almonds.
4. Serve with toast. Enjoy.


## HEALTHY POPCORN SNACK

Everyone will enjoy this yummy take on popcorn without all the butter and salt.

**Time:** 10 minutes

**Serving Size:** 1 | 2 | 4 servings

**Prep Time:** 5 minutes

**Cook Time:** 2 minutes

**Nutritional Facts/Info:**

Calories 138

Carbs 19.6 g

Fat 5.2 g

Protein 5.2 g

**Ingredients:**

- 2 tbsp | ⅓ | ⅔ cup microwave popping corn
- ½ | 1 | 2 apples (cored, diced)
- ¼ | 1 | 1 carrot (trimmed, diced)
- ¼ | 1 | 1 medium cucumber (diced)
- ½ | 1 | 2 tbsp mixed seeds like pepita, sunflower, and sesame
- 2 tbsp | ⅓ | ⅔ cup light tasty cheese (grated)
- ⅛ | ¼ | ½ tbsp thyme leaves (to serve)

**Directions:**

1. Pour corn kernels into a large paper bag, then fold top three times to tightly seal.

2. Microwave on high for 2 minutes or until popping stops.
3. Tip popcorn into a bowl and toss to cool.
4. Add the rest of the ingredients and toss.
5. Divide into bowls, then sprinkle with thyme. Enjoy.

## SPICY PUMPKIN HUMMUS WITH PITA CRISPBREAD

A delectable dip with super crunch crispbreads will stop cravings until the next meal.

**Time:** 45 minutes

**Serving Size:** 1 | 2 | 4 servings

**Prep Time:** 10 minutes

**Cook Time:** 30 minutes

**Nutritional Facts/Info:**

Calories 228

Carbs 28.5 g

Fat 10.4 g

Protein 7.6 g

**Ingredients:**

- 65 | 125 |250 g pumpkin (peeled, diced)
- Extra virgin olive oil spray
- 100 | 200 | 400 g chickpeas (rinsed, drained)
- ½ | 1 | 2 tbsp tahini
- ¼ | ½ | 1 tbsp lemon juice
- ¼ | ½ | 1 tsp ground cumin
- ¼ | ½ | 1 tsp cinnamon
- ¼ | ½ | 1 garlic clove (crushed)
- ½ | 1 | 2 tbsp fresh coriander (chopped)
- ½ | 1 | 2 wholemeal pita bread (split apart, quartered)
- ¼ | ½ | 1 tbsp extra virgin olive oil

- Paprika (to sprinkle)
- 1 tsp chili flakes (to serve)

## Directions:

1. Set oven to 350 °F/180 °C and line a baking tray with parchment paper.
2. Tip pumpkin onto the baking tray and spread out.
3. Spray lightly with oil, then roast for 25 minutes or until caramelized.
4. Remove from oven and tip the pumpkin into a food processor bowl.
5. Arrange the pita bread onto the parchment paper and brush with oil. Sprinkle with paprika.
6. Cook for 5 minutes or until crispy and the edges start to brown. Remove from oven.
7. Meanwhile, in a food processor, add the chickpeas, tahini, lemon juice, ground cumin, cinnamon, and garlic clove to the pumpkin. Season and blend until smooth.
8. Stir in fresh coriander.
9. Spoon into a bowl and sprinkle with chili flakes.
10. Serve with the pita crispbreads. Enjoy.


SALTY SWEET CRISPY SNACK

This collection of yummies has a different selection of food to dip.

**Time:** 10 minutes

**Serving Size:** 1 | 2 | 4 servings

**Prep Time:** 10 minutes

**Nutritional Facts/Info:**

Calories 149

Carbs 30.5 g

Fat 0.5 g

Protein 6 g

**Ingredients:**

- ¼ | ½ | 1 large red apple (cored, sliced)
- ¼ | ½ | 1 fennel bulb (thinly sliced)
- 25 | 50 | 100 g fresh snow peas or sugar snap peas (trimmed)
- 2 | 4 | 8 pitted prunes
- 2 tbsp | ¼ | ½ cup whole wheat pretzels
- 37 | 75 | 150 g low-fat cottage cheese with pineapple
- ¼ | ½ | 1 tsp thyme leaves (to serve)

**Directions:**

1. Arrange the fruit, vegetables, prunes, and pretzels around the cottage cheese.
2. Sprinkle the dip with thyme and serve.

NUTTY CHOCOLATE BALLS

These decadent chocolate balls taste similar to Italy's Ferrero Rocher but with half the calories. Only 36 per ball!

**Time:** 10 minutes

**Serving Size:** 1 | 2 | 4 (makes 18)

**Prep Time:** 10 minutes

**Nutritional Facts/Info:**

Calories 162

Carbs 18.4 g

Fat 9.9 g

Protein 4 g

**Ingredients:**

- 55 | 105 | 210 g pitted dates
- ¼ | ½ | 1 cup chopped hazelnuts
- ½ | 1 | 2 tbsp extra virgin avocado oil
- ½ | 1 | 2 tbsp cocoa powder
- ¼ | ½ | 1 tbsp maple syrup
- ¼ | ½ | 1 tbsp chia seeds
- A pinch | ¼ | ½ tsp ground cinnamon
- 1 tbsp | 2 tbsp | ¼ cup almond meal

## Directions:

1. Line a shallow airtight container with baking paper.
2. In a food processor or blender, add the dates, hazelnuts, oil, cacao, maple syrup, chia seeds, and cinnamon, then process until the mixture is combined and sticky.
3. Spread the almond meal on a plate.
4. Roll tablespoonfuls of the date mixture into balls then in the almond meal to coat lightly.
5. Transfer to prepared container.
6. Chill for 1 hour then serve.

CRUNCHY PUMPKIN SEEDS

These nutritious morsels are popular with crunch and munch to please. Add your favorite condiments to the recipe to spice or sweeten it up. We've even made considerations for those with air fryers!

**Time:** 50 minutes

**Serving Size:** 1 | 2 | 4 servings

**Prep Time:** 15 minutes

**Cook Time:** 35 minutes

**Nutritional Facts/Info:**

Calories 150

Carbs 3 g

Fat 12.5 g

Protein 6.8 g

**Ingredients:**

- ¾ | 1½ | 3 cups fresh pumpkin seeds (rinsed, dried)
- ½ | 1 | 2 tsp extra virgin olive oil

**Directions:**

Airfryer:

1. In a small bowl, mix the pumpkin seeds with the oil. Season.
2. Add the seeds to the air fryer basket and cook at 350 °F/180 °C for 10 minutes.
3. Remove from air fryer.

Oven:

1. Set oven to 325 °F/165 °C and line a baking tray with parchment paper.
2. Simmer pumpkin seeds in boiling water for 10 minutes.
3. Remove from pot and dry on paper towels.
4. In a small bowl, mix the pumpkin seeds with the oil. Season. (This is when to add extra flavors if desired.)
5. Spread out on baking tray in one layer, then bake for 25 minutes or until cooked to your liking.
6. Remove the tray after 10 minutes, then shake to redistribute the seeds.
7. The seeds are cooked when crispy outside and tender inside.
8. If you'd like even crispier seeds, turn the oven off and leave the seeds to sit for 30 minutes before removing. Enjoy.

## VEGAN HAZELNUT SPREAD WITH STRAWBERRIES

Homemade Nutella on toast with strawberries. Yes, please! With fewer calories, the spread stores in the fridge for up to 2 weeks.

**Time:** 35 minutes

**Serving Size:** 1 | 2 | 4 servings (makes 1 cup)

**Prep Time:** 10 minutes

**Cook Time:** 20 minutes

**Nutritional Facts/Info:**

Calories 238

Carbs 40.9 g

Fat 4.6 g

Protein 10.9 g

**Ingredients:**

- 35 | 75 | 150 g blanched hazelnuts
- 1 tbsp | 2 tbsp | ¼ cup cacao powder
- ½ | 1 | 2 tbsp maple syrup
- 1 tbsp | 2 tbsp | ¼ cup extra virgin avocado oil
- 3 | 6 | 12 strawberries (hulled, sliced)
- 1 | 2 | 4 slices wholemeal bread
- ¼ | ½ | 1 tbsp fresh mint leaves (picked, to serve)

**Directions:**

1. Set oven to 340 °F/170 °C or 300 °F/150 °C, fan forced. Line a baking tray with parchment paper.
2. Place hazelnuts on prepared tray and roast for 15-20 minutes until golden.
3. Tip the hazelnuts into a food processor or blender, then add cacao, maple syrup, and oil.

4. Blend scraping down the sides occasionally for 1–2 minutes until finely ground.
5. Add 1 tbsp | 2 tbsp | ¼ cup water, then process until thick and smooth.
6. Transfer to an airtight jar or container.
7. Toast the bread.
8. Spread the hazelnut spread over the toast, then top with strawberries.
9. Sprinkle with mint leaves and serve.

## ROASTED PEPPERS WITH HOMEMADE LABNEH

So easy to make, labneh is a low-calorie snack that can be made at home to use at any time. This recipe makes enough for 8 servings, but the nutritional information is set for 4 people, allowing for the remaining labneh to be used later.

**Time:** 10 minutes (plus overnight resting)

**Serving Size:** 1 | 2 | 4 servings

**Prep Time:** 10 minutes

**Cook Time:** 5 minutes

**Nutritional Facts/Info:**

Calories 163

Carbs 11 g

Fat 10.8 g

Protein 3.2 g

**Ingredients:**

- 250 g | 500 g | 1 kg Greek yogurt
- Extra virgin olive oil
- 10 | 20 | 40 g roasted peppers marinated in olive oil (drained)
- 10 | 20 | 40 g pitted kalamata olives (sliced)

- 2 | 4 | 8 slices whole grain ciabatta or sourdough bread
- 2 | 4 | 8 sprigs fresh basil (picked)

## Directions:

1. To make the labneh, use a clean disposable cleaning towel or dishcloth to line a bowl with the edges overhanging.
2. Spoon the yogurt into the cloth, then tie the corners up into a tight knot around a wooden spoon.
3. Transfer the ball of yogurt and bowl to the fridge. Sit the wooden spoon on items taller than the bowl, so the cloth ball is above the bowl allowing the whey to drip out.
4. Leave overnight.
5. Discard the whey in the bowl, or use it in a smoothie or soup, then remove the cloth from the labneh.
6. To use on the day as a mezze plate, transfer to a bowl and follow the appetizer recipe for labneh mezze plate.
7. To last longer, pinch off sections of labneh, then roll into balls. Place in a clean, airtight jar.
8. Add fresh herbs, chilis, etc., then cover completely with oil.
9. Toast the bread and spread with labneh.
10. Top with chargrilled peppers, then sprinkle with olives and basil. Enjoy.

APPETIZERS

Usually eaten before the main meal, served as party food, or added to an antipasto plate, a small amount of these appetizers can also be snacked on to stave off hunger between meals.

### Crab Cocktail with Avocado Sauce

Full of flavor, there won't be any leftovers from this dish!

Time: 50 minutes

**Serving Size:** 1 | 2 | 4 servings

**Prep Time:** 35 minutes

**Nutritional Facts/Info:**

Calories 235

Carbs 7 g

Fat 5.2 g

Protein 38.2 g

**Ingredients:**

- 185 | 375 | 750 g cooked snow crab leg clusters or king crab (shelled, roughly chopped)
- ¼ | ½ | 1 avocado (stoned, peeled)
- ½ | 1 | 2 tbsp lemon juice
- 65 | 125 | 250 g low-fat Greek yogurt
- ¼ | ½ | 1 large sweet pickled gherkin (chopped fine)
- ½ | 1 | 2 tsp sweet chili sauce
- ½ | 1 | 2 tsp thyme (picked)
- ½ | 1 | 2 cups iceberg lettuce (shredded)
- ¾ tsp | ¼ | ½ tbsp parsley (chopped)

**Directions:**

1. Chill the crab until ready to construct the cocktails.
2. In a small bowl, add the avocado and lemon juice, then smash together roughly. Season.
3. Add yogurt, pickles, sweet chili sauce, and thyme. Mix thoroughly with a fork.
4. In attractive parfait or cocktail glasses, sprinkle half the lettuce between the glasses.
5. Add half the crab meat.
6. Dollop the avocado sauce over the top, then repeat the layers.
7. Scatter the parsley over the top, then cover and chill. Enjoy.

## HERBED CAMEMBERT WITH SEMI-DRIED TOMATOES

Lovely as an appetizer on a hot day because the heat melts the cheese into the tomato and herbs. Delish!

**Time:** 10 minutes

**Serving Size:** 8 servings

**Prep Time:** 5 minutes

**Nutritional Facts/Info:**

Calories 92

Carbs 0.4 g

Fat 6.8 g

Protein 6.8 g

**Ingredients:**

- 250 g camembert round
- ½ cup semi-dried tomatoes (drained)
- 1 cup mixed fresh herbs like parsley, basil, thyme, rosemary, and oregano (roughly chopped)
- ⅓ cup caper berries (drained, halved)

**Directions:**

1. Sit the camembert on a serving plate.
2. With a sharp knife, slice the camembert in half lengthwise to create two halves like a sandwich.
3. Place the tomatoes on the bottom half of the round.
4. Cover with the herbs, then top with the other half of the round.
5. Press down.
6. Top with caper berries and serve with crackers.

## PICKLED VEGETABLES (GIARDINIERA)

Traditionally served as an appetizer, giardiniera can also be tossed into a salad or served on bruschetta.

**Time:** 40 minutes

**Serving Size:** 4 servings (Makes ~6¼ cups)

**Prep Time:** 20 minutes (You will need a large sterilized jar—or several smaller jars— with airtight lids for this dish.)

**Cook Time:** 5 minutes

**Nutritional Facts/Info:**

Calories 186

Carbs 23.4 g

Fat 7.9 g

Protein 3.7 g

**Ingredients:**

- ¼ medium head cauliflower (cut into small florets)
- 1 cucumber (sliced into quarters lengthwise, deseeded)
- 2 carrots (peeled, sliced into thick batons, and cut crosswise)
- 6 small red onions (peeled)
- 1 red pepper (deseeded, sliced thickly, and cut crosswise)
- 1 handful green beans (ends trimmed)
- 4 garlic cloves (peeled)
- 2 tbsp extra virgin olive oil
- 2½ cups white or red wine vinegar
- 12 black peppercorns
- 2 tsp mustard seeds
- 4 sprigs fresh thyme
- 2 bay leaves

**Directions:**

1. Line the cucumber quarters up together and cut in half crosswise.
2. Add boiling water to a medium saucepan, then add a generous pinch of salt.
3. When the salted water is boiling, gently tip the cauliflower, onions, beans, and carrots in, then blanch for 2–3 minutes until the beans and carrots brighten in color. Drain.
4. Add all the vegetables to a bowl, then pour in the oil. Stir to coat.
5. Pour some vinegar into the bottom of the jar, then layer the vegetables tightly with mustard seeds, peppercorns, thyme, and bay leaves.
6. Fill the jar with the rest of the vinegar to completely cover the vegetables.
7. Secure the lid well, then stand in a cool, dark place for at least one week before using.
8. May be kept in the fridge once opened but bring to room temperature before serving.

## MARINATED MUSHROOMS

These tasty morsels are wonderful on their own or in salads and pasta.

**Time:** 10 minutes

**Serving Size:** 1 | 2 | 4 servings

**Prep Time:** 10 minutes

**Cook Time:**

**Nutritional Facts/Info:**

Calories 232

Carbs 2.3 g

Fat 25.5 g

Protein 2 g

**Ingredients:**

- 30 | 60 | 120 g button mushrooms (thinly sliced)
- 1 | 2 | 3 tbsp lemon juice
- 2 tbsp | ¼ | ½ cup extra virgin olive oil
- ½ | 1 | 2 tbsp parsley (chopped)
- A pinch | ⅛ | ¼ tsp salt
- A pinch | ⅛ | ¼ tsp tarragon
- A pinch | ⅛ | ¼ tsp pepper

**Directions:**

1. Mix all ingredients except the mushrooms in a bowl.
2. Add mushrooms and mix well.
3. Cover and marinate for 4 hours or overnight. Enjoy.

KOFTA BALLS WITH LEMON TZATZIKI

Tasty balls of goodness to pop into your mouth are even better dipped in this lemon tzatziki.

**Time:** 30 minutes

**Serving Size:** 1 | 2 | 4 servings

**Prep Time:** 10 minutes

**Cook Time:** 10 minutes

**Nutritional Facts/Info:**

Calories 307

Carbs 12.4 g

Fat 19.4 g

Protein 22.5 g

**Ingredients:**

- 100 | 200 | 400 g lean lamb mince
- ¼ | ½ | 1 long red chili pepper (deseeded, chopped fine)
- ¼ | ½ | 1 small red onion (chopped)
- 3 tbsp | ⅜ | ¾ cup flat-leaf parsley (½ cup chopped, ¼ cup picked, to serve)
- 3 tbsp | ⅜ | ¾ cup mint leaves (½ cup chopped, ¼ cup picked, to serve)
- A pinch | ¾ | 1½ tsp ground cumin
- A pinch | ¾ | 1½ tsp ground coriander
- Extra virgin olive oil spray
- 50 | 100 | 200 g tzatziki with roasted garlic
- ¼ | ½ | 1 lemon (juiced, zested)
- ½ | 1 | 2 cups arugula rocket leaves (to serve)

**Directions:**

1. In a bowl, add mince, onion, chopped parsley and mint, cumin, coriander, and chili then stir together. Season.
2. With a plate nearby and using a tablespoon, roll small meatballs from the mixture.
3. In a frying pan on medium-high heat, spray with oil.
4. Cook kofta balls for -6 minutes, turning until caramelized and cooked through. Remove to a paper towel-lined plate.
5. Spoon the tzatziki into a dip bowl, then add the lemon juice. Stir, then sprinkle with zest. Set on a serving plate.
6. Scatter rocket over serving plate and add the koftas.
7. Dust with remaining herbs. Enjoy.

SPICY SARDINE-STUFFED CELERY

A low-calorie, spicy appetizer that won't last long at your next get-together.

**Time:** 15 minutes

**Serving Size:** Makes -24 serves

**Prep Time:** 5 minutes

**Nutritional Facts/Info:**

Calories 54

Carbs 1.3 g

Fat 4.4 g

Protein 2.1 g

**Ingredients:**

- 2 cans sardines in extra virgin olive oil with jalapeño peppers or cracked pepper (drained, reserving the oil, jalapeños, and peppers)
- 8 medium celery stalks
- 225 g low-fat cream cheese spread (at room temperature)
- ½ cup sweet red bell pepper (diced)
- 1 tsp Worcestershire sauce
- 1–2 tbsp olive oil reserved from can
- 1 tbsp fresh chives (finely chopped, to serve)

**Directions:**

1. In a small mixing bowl, combine cream cheese, bell pepper, Worcestershire sauce, reserved jalapeños, and cracked peppers.
2. Add reserved sardine oil, then mix until the ingredients are spreadable.
3. Spread mixture into the celery stalks with a knife.
4. Top with sardines, leaving a gap between each sardine for cutting.
5. Slice the stuffed celery sticks, then lay them out on a serving platter.
6. Sprinkle with chives.
7. Cover and chill until served.

## HERBED HUMMUS DIP

A delicious, versatile dip that can also be used in antipasti, pizzas, sandwiches, as a side, and so much more. You can even sprout your own chickpeas over a week at home in a sprouting jar.

**Time:** 40 minutes

**Serving Size:** 1 | 2 | 4 servings

**Prep Time:** 20 minutes

**Cook Time:** 20 minutes

**Nutritional Facts/Info:**

Calories 293

Carbs 42.9 g

Fat 9.7 g

Protein 10.4 g

**Ingredients:**

- 1 | 2 | 3 cups chickpeas (rinsed)
- ½ | 1 | 2 tbsp cold water
- 1 sml | 1 med | 1 large garlic clove (peeled, minced)
- 10 | 20 | 40 g tahini
- ¼ | ½ | 1 tbsp lemon juice
- 1 | 2 | 4 pinches salt
- ¼ | ½ | 1 tbsp extra virgin olive oil
- ⅛ | ¼ | ½ tsp cumin
- ⅓ tsp | ¼ | ½ tbsp parsley (chopped)
- ⅓ tsp | ¼ | ½ tbsp tarragon (chopped)

**Directions:**

1. Leaving 5 | 10 | 20 chickpeas in reserve for garnishing, transfer the chickpeas to a food processor fitted with a

blade, then run on high until the chickpeas resemble a fine paste.

2. Add the tahini, juice, water, and salt, then process for 4 minutes. Stir in the herbs.
3. Spoon the hummus into a serving bowl and stir the mixture.
4. Drizzle the olive oil over the top of the dip in a circular pattern, then sprinkle the reserved chickpeas around the center. Sprinkle with cumin.
5. Serve with accompaniments to dip into the mixture, like wholemeal pita bread pieces, vegetable crudites, or whole grain crackers.
6. Cover leftover dip and refrigerate to last several days.

## MEDITERRANEAN VEGGIE SLICE

Chock full of goodness and flavor, this dish is perfect for entertaining and it won't last long! Keeps well chilled in an airtight container. Reheat before eating. Swap out the flour for gluten-free varieties if you're coeliac.

**Time:** 1 hour 15 minutes

**Serving Size:** 12 servings

**Prep Time:** 35 minutes

**Cook Time:** 40 minutes

**Nutritional Facts/Info:**

Calories 235

Carbs 13.9 g

Fat 13.6 g

Protein 14.9 g

**Ingredients:**

- 2 large zucchini (grated into a clean kitchen cloth over a bowl,

then drained by grabbing the cloth corners and squeezing out the liquid several times)
- 1 carrot (grated)
- 1 onion (finely chopped)
- 1 cup low-fat cheddar cheese (grated)
- 1 cup wholemeal self-raising flour
- ½ cup extra virgin olive oil
- 200 g cherry tomatoes (halved)
- 5 free-range eggs (lightly beaten)
- 125 g corn kernels (rinsed, drained)
- 1 capsicum (diced)
- ½ cup mushrooms (diced)
- ½ cup sliced kalamata olives
- 50 g baby spinach leaves
- ½ cup fresh basil leaves (chopped)
- 12 tomato slices
- 60 g low-fat feta cheese (crumbled)
- ½ cup parmesan cheese (shredded)
- Fresh rosemary sprigs (to serve)

## Directions:

1. Set oven to 350 °F/180 °C and line a lasagne, casserole dish, or small baking tray with parchment paper.
2. Add all ingredients to a bowl and mix thoroughly.
3. Spread mixture into prepared dish and firm down.
4. Top with tomato slices in a 4 x 3-row pattern (so they don't get sliced).
5. Sprinkle the tomato slices with crumbled feta cheese.
6. Sprinkle the rest with parmesan.
7. Bake for 40 minutes until the top is golden brown.
8. Cool slightly before cutting in the pan.
9. Top each piece with a generous sprig of rosemary. Enjoy. (Can be served at room temperature.)

## NUTTY DATE GRISSINO

Something different that's so enjoyable and tasty to eat.

**Time:** 10 minutes

**Serving Size:** Makes 16

**Prep Time:** 10 minutes

**Nutritional Facts/Info:**

Calories 136

Carbs 18.7 g

Fat 6.5 g

Protein 3.2 g

**Ingredients:**

- 1 cup toasted sliced almonds
- 12 medjool dates (pitted, roughly chopped)
- ¾ cup whole grain rolled oats
- 2 tbsp almond spread
- 1 tbsp cacao
- 16 seeded whole wheat grissini breadsticks

**Directions:**

1. In a food processor or blender, add half the almonds, dates, oats, and almond spread, then blend until it turns pasty.
2. Chop remaining almonds finely and spread on a plate.
3. Wrap 1 tbsp of date paste around one end of each breadstick, pressing firmly.
4. Roll the sticks in chopped almonds to coat. Enjoy.

## NUTTY CHICKPEA CRISPIES

Salty, sweet, and crispy, this appetizer is absolutely scrumptious.

**Time:** 55 minutes

**Serving Size:** 1 | 2 | 4 servings

**Prep Time:** 5 minutes

**Cook Time:** 45 minutes

**Nutritional Facts/Info:**

Calories 225

Carbs 28.6 g

Fat 11.6 g

Protein 4.9 g

**Ingredients:**

- 100 |200 | 400 g canned chickpeas (rinsed, drained)
- 37 | 75 | 150 g blanched almonds
- ½ | 1 | 2 tbsp extra virgin olive oil
- ½ | 1 | 2 tsp smoky paprika
- ¼ | ½ | 1 tsp curry powder
- ½ | 1 | 2 tsp sea salt flakes
- ½ | 1 | 2 tsp dried oregano
- ¾ | 1½ | 3 tsp pure honey

**Directions:**

1. Set oven to 350 °F/180 °C. Line an oven tray with parchment paper.
2. Dry chickpeas thoroughly with paper towel, then add to a bowl with almonds.
3. Add half the oil and toss to coat.
4. Add paprika, curry powder, and 1 tsp of salt flakes, then shake

well.

5. Spread out on tray, then bake for 45 minutes, turning every 15 minutes until golden. Remove and set aside.
6. Meanwhile, in a small saucepan over low heat, add oregano, honey, and remaining oil then stir.
7. Add chickpeas and almonds, then toss to cover.
8. Return to oven tray, dust with remaining salt, then bake for 10–15 minutes until crispy and caramelized.
9. Cool on tray. Enjoy.

## GREEK TOASTY APPETIZERS

Crunchy whole grain, seeded toast with olives and cheese. What's not to love?

**Time:** 20 minutes

**Serving Size:** 16 servings

**Prep Time:** 5 minutes

**Cook Time:** 10 minutes

**Nutritional Facts/Info:**

Calories 73

Carbs 11.4 g

Fat 2.3 g

Protein 3.7 g

**Ingredients:**

- 8 slices wholemeal seeded sprouted bread
- Extra virgin olive oil (to drizzle)
- 1 cup pitted kalamata olives (sliced)
- 2 cups low-fat mozzarella cheese (shredded)
- 2 spring onions (sliced)
- 2 tbsp basil (chopped)

## Directions:

1. Turn on grill and line grilling tray with parchment paper.
2. Spread the sliced bread onto the tray. Drizzle with oil. Season.
3. Pop into oven and grill until toasted. Remove.
4. Sprinkle each slice with olives, then top with mozzarella.
5. Slide into the oven again and grill until the cheese is melted.
6. Remove and sit for a minute.
7. Slice each piece in half crossways.
8. Arrange on a serving plate and scatter with spring onions and basil. Enjoy.

LABNEH MEZZE PLATE

In Turkey and Greece, mezze plates are popular with a glorious selection of food put together for a crowd to enjoy. Much like tapas in Spain, or meze in Italy, these little bowls of deliciousness are made to be relished.

**Time:** 15 minutes

**Serving Size:** 1 | 2 | 4 servings

**Prep Time:** 10 minutes

**Nutritional Facts/Info:**

Calories 248

Carbs 18.9 g

Fat 15.3 g

Protein 5.7 g

**Ingredients:**

- 75 | 150 | 300 g labneh (see recipe for roasted peppers with homemade labneh)
- Extra virgin olive oil (to drizzle)
- ¼ | ½ | 1 lemon (juiced, zested)
- ⅛ | ¼ | ½ cucumber (sliced lengthwise with a peeler)
- 2 tbsp | ¼ | ½ cup mixed olives
- 2 tbsp | ¼ | ½ cup mixed heirloom cherry tomatoes (halved)
- ¼ | ½ | 1 tsp sumac
- ¼ | ½ | 1 tsp chili flakes
- ¼ | ½ | 1 tbsp fresh basil leaves (chopped)
- ¼ | ½ | 1 tsp fresh thyme leaves
- ¼ | ½ | 1 tbsp fresh dill
- ¼ | ½ | 1 tbsp fresh mint leaves
- ½ | 1 | 2 wholemeal pita bread (quartered)

**Directions:**

1. Transfer the labneh to the middle of a medium-deep bowl and season. Drizzle with oil and lemon juice.
2. Sprinkle with lemon zest, sumac, and chili flakes across the center.
3. Arrange the cucumber, olives, and tomatoes around the edge, making a colorful display.
4. Sprinkle with herbs.
5. Transfer bowl to a plate and serve with pita bread.

## PRAWN AND VEGGIE STICKS

This no-cook appetizer is easy to eat anytime and full of nutritious, great flavor.

**Time:** 45 minutes

**Serving Size:** Makes 12

**Prep Time:** 25 minutes

**Nutritional Facts/Info:**

Calories 94

Carbs 10 g

Fat 2.6 g

Protein 7 g

**Ingredients:**

- 12 kebab sticks (10 in/25 cm)
- 750 g cooked prawns (shelled, deveined)
- 1 green capsicum pepper (deseeded, cut into 12 chunks)
- 3 pineapple rings (quartered)
- 12 large black pitted olives
- 12 cherry tomatoes
- 100 g feta (cut into 12 cubes)

**Directions:**

1. Ensure all ingredients are on hand and that a serving plate is ready.
2. Thread the ingredients, one at a time, onto each stick, piercing the prawn twice through each end until all sticks have 6 pieces.
3. Enjoy.

## ROAST PUMPKIN GNOCCHI WITH CRISPY SAGE

A delicious take on traditional potato gnocchi with fewer calories and more flavor.

**Time:** 1 hour 5 minutes

**Serving Size:** 1 | 2 | 4 servings

**Prep Time:** 5 minutes

**Cook Time:** 40 minutes

**Nutritional Facts/Info:**

Calories 270

Carbs 31.7 g

Fat 12.3 g

Protein 11 g

**Ingredients:**

- 185 | 375 | 750 g pumpkin (peeled, cut into 1 in/3 cm chunks)
- 1 tbsp | 2 tbsp | ¼ cup finely grated parmesan (plus extra to serve)
- ⅓ | ⅔ | 1¼ cup wholemeal flour (plus extra)
- 1 tbsp | 2 tbsp | ¼ cup extra virgin olive oil
- ½ | 1 | 2 cloves garlic (crushed)
- 2 tbsp | ¼ | ½ cup sage leaves
- 1¼ tbsp | 2½ tbsp | ⅓ cup pine nuts

**Directions:**

1. Set oven to 430 °F/220 °C or 400 °F/200 °C, fan forced. Line a baking tray with parchment paper.
2. Spread pumpkin in a single layer on tray and season.
3. Bake for 35 minutes until golden and tender.

4. Tip into a large bowl, mash until smooth, then stir in parmesan.
5. Stir in 1 cup flour, ½ cup at a time until a firm, slightly sticky dough forms. If too sticky, add a little more flour 1 tbsp at a time.
6. Divide dough into 1 | 2 | 4 portions.
7. Lightly flour a clean cutting board and roll the dough into a ¾ in/2 cm thick log.
8. Using a lightly floured knife, cut logs into ¾ in/2 cm pieces.
9. Gently press gnocchi with the back of a floured fork.
10. Prepare a large saucepan of boiling, salted water, then add the gnocchi to boil for 2 minutes or until they float.
11. Drain and transfer to serving plates.
12. Meanwhile, heat a small frying pan over medium heat, then add the oil.
13. Add the garlic and sage, then sauté shaking pan for 2 minutes or until the sage is crispy.
14. Drizzle the gnocchi with garlic oil.
15. Sprinkle with crispy sage, pine nuts, and extra parmesan. Enjoy.

## GRILLED CALAMARI WITH RADICCHIO

Tender and crispy, this recipe has instructions for both fresh and frozen squid.

**Time:** 20–45 minutes (plus marinating time)

**Serving Size:** 1 | 2 | 4 servings

**Prep Time:** Frozen 30 minutes. Fresh 15 minutes.

**Cook Time:** 6 minutes

**Nutritional Facts/Info:**

Calories 172

Carbs 15.4 g

Fat 4.8 g

Protein 17 g

**Ingredients:**

- 100 | 200 | 400 g fresh medium squid (or frozen tubes, sliced down one side)
- ¾ | 1½ | 3 soft kiwifruit (peeled, mashed)
- ¼ | ½ | 1 cup radicchio leaves (chopped)
- ¼ | ½ | 1 1 cup mixed baby salad leaves
- 1 tbsp | 2 tbsp | ¼ cup pistachio nuts (shelled, chopped)
- 2 tbsp | ¼ | ½ cup balsamic dressing
- 2 tbsp | ¼ | ½ tbsp pure honey
- ¼ | ½ | 1 tsp chili flakes (to serve)
- ¼ | ½ | 1 tbsp lemon thyme (picked, to serve)

**Directions:**

For fresh squid:

1. Gently pull the head off the squid.
2. Using a sharp knife, slice the tentacles off the body.
3. Slice the wings off the side of the body and remove the hard cartilage you can feel with your fingers.
4. Slice the body down one side and flatten.
5. Scrape anything off the inside of the squid so there's only flesh left.
6. Scrape the edge to find the fine membrane, then strip it off and discard. Continue below.

For frozen tubes:

1. Score the flat pieces of squid finely in a diagonal direction both ways.
2. Cut into large bite-sized pieces and tip into a glass bowl.
3. Add the kiwifruit and mix together. Cover and chill for 1 hour or overnight.

4. In a medium bowl, mix the radicchio with the salad leaves and pistachios. Set aside.
5. In a screw-top jar, add the dressing, honey, and thyme, then shake well.
6. Rinse the kiwifruit off the squid, then pat dry with paper towel. Season.
7. Heat a chargrill pan or barbeque plate and fry the squid for 3 minutes each side until tender and caramelized.
8. Remove to a paper towel-lined plate.
9. Scatter on a serving plate and add the salad.
10. Drizzle with the dressing. Sprinkle with chili flakes and thyme. Enjoy.

# CHAPTER 5
# BREAKFAST RECIPES

BREAKFAST

## *Fluffy Berry Pancakes*

The whole family will love these healthy ricotta pancakes for breakfast. Perfect for the weekend.

**Time:** 45 minutes

**Serving Size:** 1 | 2 | 4 servings

**Prep Time:** 25 minutes

**Cook Time:** 20 minutes

**Nutritional Facts/Info:**

Calories 299

Carbs 36.6 g

Fat 11.7 g

Protein 13 g

## Ingredients:

- ½ | 1 | 2 cups whole wheat plain flour
- ½ | 1 | 2 tsp baking powder
- 1 | 2 | 4 free-range eggs
- 6 tbsp | ¾ | 1½ cups unsweetened almond milk
- ½ | 1 | 2 tsp pure honey
- A pinch | ¼ | ½ tsp cinnamon
- 5 tbsp | 10 tbsp | 1¼ cups low-fat ricotta
- Extra virgin olive oil spray
- 65 | 125 | 250 g blueberries
- A drop | ¼ | ½ tsp vanilla bean paste
- 2 | 4 | 8 fresh lemon thyme sprigs (to serve)
- 1 | 2 | 4 fresh basil sprigs (to serve)

## Directions:

1. In a large bowl, mix the flour and baking powder together.
2. In a separate bowl, whisk the eggs, almond milk, honey, and 3 tbsp | 6 tbsp | ¾ cup ricotta.
3. Add the egg mixture to the flour mixture, then gently stir until just combined.
4. Set aside to rest for 15 minutes until bubbles form in the mixture.
5. Heat a large frying pan over medium-low heat and spray lightly with oil.
6. Spoon ⅓ cup batter into the pan and spread to form a circle that takes up less than half of the pan (around 5 in/12 cm). Scatter 10 blueberries over the pancake.
7. Repeat to make a second pancake in the pan.
8. Cook for several minutes until the pancakes are browning on the bottom. (Check with an egg flip.)
9. Flip the pancakes over and continue to cook until golden and cooked through.
10. Transfer to a plate next to the stove and cover to keep warm (or place in the oven on lowest heat).

11. Spray the pan again with oil, then repeat the process to make 12 pancakes.

12. Meanwhile, in a small saucepan over medium heat, add ⅓ cup water and the remaining blueberries, then bring to a boil. Cook until the blueberries begin to soften. Remove from the heat.

13. Mix the remaining ricotta with the vanilla bean paste and set aside.

14. Divide pancakes among serving plates in fanned stacks of 3.

15. Dollop each with vanilla ricotta, then spoon over the blueberry mixture.

16. Garnish with lemon thyme and basil sprigs. Enjoy.

### *Salsa Bruschetta with Poached Egg*

A filling dish like this is a wonderful way to start the day full of energy.

**Time:** 35 minutes

**Serving Size:** 1 | 2 | 4 servings

**Prep Time:** 20 minutes

**Cook Time:** 15 minutes

**Nutritional Facts/Info:**

Calories 206

Carbs 21.3 g

Fat 8.3 g

Protein 10.8 g

**Ingredients:**

- 1 | 2 | 4 large tomatoes (diced)
- ¼ | ½ | 1 red onion (diced)
- ¼ | ½ | 1 tbsp parsley (chopped)
- ¼ | ½ | 1 tbsp balsamic vinegar

- 1 | 2 | 4 free-range eggs
- 1 tsp white vinegar
- 1 | 2 | 4 slices wholemeal or whole grain bread like sourdough or ciabatta (thickly sliced)
- ¼ | ½ | 1 tbsp extra virgin olive oil
- ½ | 1 | 2 cloves garlic cut in half
- 1 | 2 | 4 fresh basil sprigs (to serve)

## Directions:

1. Add the tomatoes, onions, and parsley to a bowl and mix.
2. Season and allow to sit for 5 minutes.
3. Add the balsamic vinegar, then set aside.
4. Add boiling water to a frying pan for poaching. Pour in the vinegar and bring to a boil.
5. Turn down the heat until gently simmering.
6. In the meantime, brush the bread with oil, then toast under the griller until golden. Turn over and continue toasting until golden.
7. Take the toast out of the oven and rub with garlic. Discard the leftover garlic.
8. Swirl the frying pan water with a spoon, then crack the eggs into the pan one at a time.
9. Use an egg flip to gently slide under the eggs to ensure they don't stick to the pan.
10. For soft eggs, cook for 2–3 minutes or 3–4 minutes for firm eggs.
11. Remove the eggs onto a plate lined with paper towel.
12. Arrange the toast on 4 serving plates, then top with salsa.
13. Gently lift the poached eggs and place on top of the salsa.
14. Crack black pepper over each egg, then garnish with basil. Enjoy.

### *Grilled Portobellos with Herby Cheese*

If you're a mushroom lover, you'll enjoy this healthy breakfast.

**Time:** 20 minutes

**Serving Size:** 1 | 2 | 4 servings

**Prep Time:** 10 minutes

**Cook Time:** 10 minutes

**Nutritional Facts/Info:**

Calories 200

Carbs 10.7 g

Fat 15.5 g

Protein 9.3 g

**Ingredients:**

- 1 tbsp | 2 tbsp | ¼ cup extra virgin olive oil
- ¼ | ½ | 1 garlic clove (crushed)
- ¼ | ½ | 1 tbsp rosemary (picked, chopped finely)
- ¼ | ½ | 1 tsp fresh thyme leaves
- ¼ | ½ | 1 lemon (juiced, zested)
- 1 | 2 | 4 portobello mushrooms (stems trimmed)
- 10 | 20 | 40 g feta cheese (crumbled)
- ¼ | ½ | 1 tbsp parmesan (grated)
- ½ | 1 | 2 tbsp low-fat mozzarella (grated)
- ¼ | ½ | 1 tsp sesame seeds (to serve)
- ¼ | ½ | 1 tbsp fresh flat leaf parsley (picked)

**Directions:**

1. Set the broiler or grill to high heat.
2. In a small bowl or jug, combine the olive oil, garlic, rosemary, thyme, lemon juice, and zest.
3. Mix the 3 cheeses together in another small bowl.
4. Place mushrooms stem side down on grill tray, then brush with the herbed oil. Grill for 3 minutes.

5. Turn the mushrooms over and pour the remaining oil into the center, distributing evenly between the mushrooms.
6. Sprinkle with mixed cheese.
7. Grill for further 3–4 minutes until mushrooms are just cooked through and the cheese has melted and turned golden.
8. Season the mushrooms with pepper, then sprinkle with sesame seeds and parsley. Enjoy.

### Turmeric Quinoa with Fruit and Nuts

This dish is so easy to eat and has wonderful Moroccan overtones. It pairs beautifully with the fruit.

**Time:** 25 minutes

**Serving Size:** 1 | 2 | 4 servings

**Prep Time:** 10 minutes

**Cook Time:** 10 minutes

**Nutritional Facts/Info:**

Calories 306

Carbs 40.7 g

Fat 14.2 g

Protein 5.5 g

**Ingredients:**

- ½ | 1 | 1¾ cup quinoa flakes
- ¾ | 1½ | 3 cups unsweetened almond milk
- 1 | 2 | 4 medjool dates (pitted, chopped)
- ½ | 1 | 2 tsp vanilla extract
- ¼ | ½ | 1 tsp ground cinnamon (plus extra to serve)
- ¼ | ½ | 1 tsp ground turmeric
- ¼ | ½ | 1 tbs almond spread
- ½ | 1 | 2 pears (cored, sliced thinly)

- ¼ | ½ | 1 banana (peeled, sliced thinly)
- ½ | 1 | 2 tbsp toasted coconut flakes (to serve)
- 8 | 15 | 30 g macadamia nuts (to serve)

## Directions:

1. In a frying pan over medium heat, toast quinoa flakes for 4 minutes, stirring often.
2. Stir in milk, ⅜ | ¾ | 1½ cups water, dates, vanilla, cinnamon, and turmeric.
3. Bring to a simmer, then reduce heat to medium-low and stir for 4 minutes until thick and creamy.
4. Stir in the almond spread.
5. Divide among serving bowls and top with the fruit.
6. Sprinkle with coconut and macadamias.
7. Finish off with dustings of the extra cinnamon and serve.

### *Summer Chia Puddings*

A refreshing, healthy cup of sunny goodness that will please anyone who eats it.

**Time:** 15 minutes

**Serving Size:** 1 | 2 | 4 servings

**Prep Time:** 15 minutes

**Nutritional Facts/Info:**

Calories 194

Carbs 21.5 g

Fat 12.5 g

Protein 7 g

**Ingredients:**

- 2 tbsp | ¼ | ½ cup white chia seeds

- ½ | 1 | 2 cups unsweetened almond milk
- ¼ | ½ | 1 tbsp maple syrup
- ½ | 1 | 2 mangoes (peeled, stoned)
- 35 | 65 | 125 g fresh raspberries
- 1 tbsp | 2 tbsp | ¼ cup pepita seeds
- ½ | 1 | 2 tsp lemon thyme (picked)

**Directions:**

1. In a medium bowl, stir the chia seeds, almond milk, and maple syrup together.
2. Refrigerate for 2 hours until thickened or overnight if preferred.
3. Cut the flesh from 1 mango, then process in a blender until smooth.
4. In 1 cup capacity glasses, add a tablespoonful of the chia mixture. Follow with a dollop of the mango puree.
5. Top with a few raspberries, then repeat the layers.
6. Cut remaining mango into ½ in/1 cm pieces.
7. Top each pudding with diced mango and remaining raspberries rising above the top of the glass.
8. Sprinkle with pepitas and thyme leaves. Enjoy.

### *Smoked Salmon on English Muffins*

A simple yet satisfying start to the day packed with vitamins.

**Time:** 20 minutes

**Serving Size:** 1 | 2 | 4 servings

**Prep Time:** 10 minutes

**Cook Time:** 10 minutes

**Nutritional Facts/Info:**

Calories 268

Carbs 33.4 g

Fat 8.6 g

Protein 13.3 g

**Ingredients:**

- 1 | 2 | 4 wholemeal English muffins (halved)
- 30 | 60 | 125 g light cream cheese spread
- 1 | 2 | 4 tomatoes (sliced)
- 2 | 4 | 8 slices of sliced smoked salmon
- Lemon juice (to serve)
- ¼ | ½ | 1 tbsp chopped fresh chives (to serve)
- 1 | 2 | 4 fresh basil leaves (to serve)

**Directions:**

1. Toast the muffins under the grill until golden. Turn over and continue to toast until cooked.
2. Spread each muffin half with cream cheese spread.
3. Add a few pieces of tomato to each muffin. Season.
4. Place the sliced salmon on a paper towel and squeeze a little lemon juice over.
5. Fold a piece of smoked salmon on top of each muffin.
6. Sprinkle with chives and basil. Enjoy.

### *Breakfast Banana Bread*

A moist, tasty bread to have with your morning cuppa that will keep you energized.

**Time:** 50 minutes

**Serving Size:** 6

**Prep Time:** 10 minutes

**Cook Time:** 35 minutes

**Nutritional Facts/Info:**

Calories 292

Carbs 33.5 g

Fat 14.6 g

Protein 8.3 g

**Ingredients:**

- ¾ cup almond meal
- 1 cup wholemeal self-raising flour
- 1 tsp cinnamon
- 1 cup sultanas
- ½ cup chopped walnuts
- 1 tbsp chia seeds
- ¼ cup extra virgin olive oil
- 2 free-range eggs (whisked)
- 1 tsp vanilla extract
- 3 bananas (overripe, mashed)
- 2 tbsp flaked almonds

**Directions:**

1. Set oven to 300 °F/150 °C. Grease and line a loaf pan with parchment paper, leaving an overhang on each side.
2. In a large bowl, add the almond meal, flour, cinnamon, sultanas, chopped walnuts, and chia seeds. Mix together.
3. Combine the oil, eggs, and vanilla essence with the mashed bananas, then pour into the dry ingredients. Mix until just combined.
4. Tip the bread mix into the loaf pan, then cover the top with flaked almonds.
5. Bake for 35 minutes or until a skewer comes out clean.
6. Cool on a wire rack before lifting the bread out of the tin with the parchment paper.
7. Add to a serving plate and slice thickly to serve.

### *Savory Oats with Crispy Veggies*

A novel yet pleasing way to change up oats into a scrumptious and healthy savory breakfast.

**Time:** 30 minutes

**Serving Size:** 1 | 2 | 4 servings

**Prep Time:** 10 minutes

**Cook Time:** 15 minutes

**Nutritional Facts/Info:**

Calories 225

Carbs 22.6 g

Fat 11.4 g

Protein 12 g

**Ingredients:**

- ½ | 1 | 2 tsp extra virgin olive oil
- ½ | 1 | 2 cups whole grain rolled oats
- ¾ | 1½ | 3 cups vegetable stock (made with boiling water)
- 1 | 2 | 4 pieces of dried porcini (chopped, steeped in a glass of warm water)
- ¼ | ½ | 1 cup red cabbage (finely shredded)
- ½ | 1 | 2 tsp ginger (grated)
- 25 | 50 | 100 g snow peas (trimmed, sliced finely)
- 10 | 20 | 40 g baby spinach leaves
- 1 | 2 | 4 free-range eggs
- ¼ | ½ | 1 tbsp sesame seeds (toasted)
- ½ | 1 | 2 tbsp chopped fresh chives (to serve)
- Extra virgin olive oil (drizzled, to serve)

**Directions:**

1. Heat a saucepan to medium, then heat the olive oil.
2. Add oats and stir for 5 minutes until lightly toasted.
3. Whisk hot vegetable stock, ginger, and porcini with steeping juice, then stir into the oats.
4. Reduce heat and simmer for 10 minutes until tender and thickened, stirring occasionally.
5. Meanwhile, in a small saucepan, heat some water for the eggs.
6. Add the eggs to warm water, then bring to a boil. Cook for 6 minutes, then drain.
7. Peel eggs when cool enough.
8. Divide the oat mixture between serving bowls.
9. Add vegetables in bunches and halved boiled eggs.
10. Sprinkle with sesame seeds and chives.
11. Drizzle lightly with extra virgin olive oil. Enjoy.

### *Garlic Mushrooms with Crusty Bread*

A classic dish with beautiful flavors that can be served from a platter or piled onto individual plates. The mushroom variety can be substituted for the type you have on hand.

**Time:** 45 minutes

**Serving Size:** 1 | 2 | 4 servings

**Prep Time:** 15 minutes

**Cook Time:** 25 minutes

**Nutritional Facts/Info:**

Calories 209

Carbs 23.5 g

Fat 9.2 g

Protein 9.4 g

**Ingredients:**

- ¾ | 1½ | 3 tbsp extra virgin olive oil
- ¼ | ½ | 1 medium onion (diced)
- 1 | 2 | 4 cloves garlic (minced)
- 75 | 150 | 300 g Swiss brown mushrooms (quartered)
- 75 | 150 | 300 g portobello mushrooms (thick sliced)
- 1 | 2 | 4 cups baby spinach leaves
- 2 tbsp | ¼ | ½ cup fresh basil leaves (torn)
- 1 tbsp | 2 tbsp | ¼ cup parmigiano reggiano parmesan (shaved with a vegetable peeler)
- 1 | 2 | 4 slices wholemeal wholegrain bread
- 2 tbsp | ¼ | ½ cup flat-leaf parsley (picked)

## Directions:

1. In a large high-sided frying pan, heat the oil over medium heat.
2. Add the garlic and onion, then sauté for 3 minutes until translucent.
3. Add the mushrooms and cook, stirring occasionally for 15 minutes until the mushrooms are tender and slightly shrunken.
4. Add the spinach and basil, then toss until starting to wilt. Cook for 2 more minutes.
5. Season to taste and remove from heat.
6. Toast the bread.
7. Transfer the mushroom mixture to a serving platter or individual plates.
8. Sprinkle the parmesan and parsley over the mushrooms, then serve immediately with the toast.

### *Poached Egg with Chargrilled Asparagus and Halloumi*

A delightfully delicious yet light breakfast fit for champions.

**Time:** 25 minutes

**Serving Size:** 1 | 2 | 4 servings

**Prep Time:** 10 minutes

**Cook Time:** 15 minutes

**Nutritional Facts/Info:**

Calories 215

Carbs 1.9 g

Fat 15.6 g

Protein 16.9 g

**Ingredients:**

- 3 | 6 | 12 asparagus spears (snapped off at the soft end)
- Extra virgin olive oil spray
- 1 | 2 | 4 slices prosciutto
- 1 | 2 | 4 slices halloumi
- 1 tsp white vinegar
- 1 | 2 | 4 free-range eggs
- ¼ | ½ | 1 tbsp extra virgin olive oil
- Shaved parmesan (to serve)
- Fresh parsley (to serve)

**Directions:**

1. Spray a frying pan with oil and heat on medium-high.
2. Add the prosciutto and cook for several minutes, turning once.
3. Remove from the pan when cooked, then place on a plate lined with a paper towel and set aside.
4. Add boiling water to a frying pan for poaching. Pour in the vinegar and bring to a boil.
5. Turn down the heat until a gentle roll in the water is achieved.
6. Meanwhile, add the asparagus and halloumi to the pan and cook, turning occasionally until lightly caramelized.
7. Remove from the pan, cut the halloumi pieces in half, then place on a plate lined with paper towel.
8. Swirl the frying pan water with a spoon, then crack the eggs into the pan one at a time.

9. Use an egg flip to gently slide under the eggs to ensure they don't stick to the pan.
10. For soft eggs, cook for 2–3 minutes or 3–4 minutes for firm eggs.
11. Remove the eggs onto another plate lined with paper towel.
12. Crumble the cooked prosciutto until shards form.
13. Arrange the asparagus together onto 4 serving plates.
14. Top the center of the asparagus piles with a poached egg.
15. Place the halloumi on the outside of the asparagus pile.
16. Drizzle the olive oil lightly across the food and around the plate.
17. Crack black pepper over the top, then sprinkle with the prosciutto shards, parmesan, and parsley. Serve immediately.

### *Crunchy Cranberry Cookies*

A nutritious way to start the day with each cookie only having 19 calories. Handy to use for snacks and lunch boxes, too.

**Time:** 50 minutes

**Serving Size:** 1 | 2 | 4 servings (makes ~18)

**Prep Time:** 10 minutes

**Cook Time:** 25 minutes

**Nutritional Facts/Info:**

Calories 342

Carbs 52 g

Fat 12 g

Protein 9.5 g

**Ingredients:**

- ½ | 1 | 2 cups whole grain rolled oats
- A pinch | ¼ | ½ tsp ground cinnamon

- 2 tbsp | ⅛ | ¼ cup cranberries
- ½ | 1 | 2 tbsp pepita seeds
- ½ | 1 | 2 tbsp hemp seeds (plus extra to serve)
- 2 tbsp | ⅛ | ¼ cup maple syrup
- 2½ tbsp | ⅓ | ⅔ cup unsalted cashew spread
- ½ | 1 | 2 ripe bananas (peeled, mashed in a bowl)

## Directions:

1. Set oven to 350 °F/180 °C and line 2 baking trays with parchment paper.
2. In a bowl, mix the oats, cinnamon, raisins, cranberries, pepitas, and hemp seeds.
3. Stir the maple syrup and cashew spread into the bowl of mashed banana and mix well.
4. Stir the mashed banana mixture into the dry ingredients and mix until well combined.
5. Using 2 tbsp of mixture for each cookie, spoon onto trays and press into a round shape, leaving a 2 in/5 cm space between each cookie.
6. Sprinkle the extra hemp seeds over the cookies.
7. Bake for 20–25 minutes or until edges are slightly browned.
8. Cool on trays, then store in an airtight container for up to 5 days.

### *Low Fat Breakfast Hash*

This colorful dish is a wonderful weekend offering that can be served in the pan for convenience and dished out at the table. Don't forget to put a chopping board under the pan to protect the table.

**Time:** 40 minutes

**Serving Size:** 1 | 2 | 4 servings

**Prep Time:** 15 minutes

**Cook Time:** 20 minutes

**Nutritional Facts/Info:**

Calories 243

Carbs 33 g

Fat 8.4 g

Protein 10.6 g

**Ingredients:**

- ¼ | ½ | 1 tbsp extra virgin olive oil
- ¼ | ½ | 1 red onion (chopped)
- 125 | 250 | 500 g sweet potato (peeled, cut into small chunks)
- ¼ | ½ | 1 red capsicum (deseeded, chopped)
- ½ | 1 | 2 garlic cloves (crushed)
- ½ | 1 | 2 zucchini (cut into chunks)
- 1½ | 3 | 6 yellow squash (the small variety with scalloped edges, halved)
- ½ | 1 | 2 cups baby spinach leaves
- 1 | 2 | 4 free-range eggs
- 1 tbsp | 2 tbsp | ¼ cup fresh oregano leaves
- 1 tbsp | 2 tbsp | ¼ cup fresh tarragon leaves
- A pinch | ½ | 1 tsp of dried chili flakes

**Directions:**

1. In a large nonstick frying pan over medium-high, heat the oil.
2. Sauté the onion, stirring for several minutes until golden.
3. Add the sweet potato, capsicum, and garlic. Cook for 10 minutes, shaking the pan occasionally until golden.
4. Add the zucchini and yellow squash, then cover the pan. Cook for 5 minutes or until the veggies are tender.
5. Add the baby spinach leaves and stir gently to incorporate.
6. Using a serving spoon, make 4 indents in the vegetable mixture and crack an egg into each one.
7. Cover the pan and cook until the eggs are done to your liking.
8. Sprinkle with herb leaves and chili flakes. Enjoy.

### *Coffee Chia Puddings with 3 Fruits*

It's easy to make these puddings after dinner and chill them overnight, ready to eat in the morning. Then all they need the next day is fresh fruit.

**Time:** 5 minutes

**Serving Size:** 1 | 2 | 4 servings

**Prep Time:** 5 minutes

**Nutritional Facts/Info:**

Calories 266

Carbs 39.7 g

Fat 8.6 g

Protein 13 g

**Ingredients:**

- ½ | 1 | 2 cups unsweetened almond milk
- ½ | 1 | 2 cups low-fat Greek yogurt
- ⅓ | ⅔ | 1⅓ cup whole grain rolled oats
- 1 | 2 | 4 tbsp chia seeds
- 1 | 2 | 4 tsp instant coffee
- ⅛ | ¼ | ½ tsp cardamom
- ⅛ | ¼ | ½ tsp cinnamon
- ½ | 1 | 2 tangerines (segmented)
- ½ | 1 | 2 fresh figs (quartered)
- 1 | 2 | 4 pitted prunes
- ½ | 1 | 2 tbsp hazelnuts (roughly chopped)

**Directions:**

1. In a large bowl, mix the milk and yogurt together.
2. Stir in the oats, chia seeds, coffee, and spices.

3. Divide into serving bowls, cover with plastic wrap, and refrigerate overnight.
4. To serve, lay out the fruit over the puddings.

### *Whole Grain Egg and Asparagus Tarts*

These delicious morsels are a nutritious breakfast and also handy to take on a picnic.

**Time:** 25 minutes

**Serving Size:** 1 | 2 | 4 servings

**Prep Time:** 5 minutes

**Cook Time:** 15 minutes

**Nutritional Facts/Info:**

Calories 284

Carbs 24.2 g

Fat 15.3 g

Protein 14.3 g

**Ingredients:**

- Extra virgin olive oil spray
- 1 | 2 | 4 whole grain wholemeal bread crusts
- ½ | 1 | 2 tbsp tomato paste
- ½ | 1 | 2 tbsp extra virgin olive oil
- ½ | 1 | 2 tbsp caramelized onions
- 1 | 2 | 4 asparagus spears (trimmed, chopped)
- 1 | 2 | 4 large free-range eggs
- 25 | 50 | 100 g baby spinach leaves (to serve)
- Balsamic glaze (to drizzle)
- ½ | 1 | 2 tbsp chopped fresh chives (to serve)
- ½ | 1 | 2 tbsp chopped fresh basil (to serve)

## Directions:

1. Set oven to 350 °F/180 °C and spray 1 | 2 | 4 large muffin tin holes with the olive oil spray.
2. Spread the tomato paste onto each piece of bread.
3. Push bread crusts into muffin tin holes, then brush the exposed edges with oil.
4. Drop ½ tbsp of caramelized onions onto the bread and push down.
5. Add a portion of the chopped asparagus on top of each tart.
6. Crack an egg into each hole, then place in the middle of the oven.
7. Bake for about 15 minutes until the egg is just cooked, then remove from the oven.
8. Set out on bread plates with a side of scattered baby spinach leaves.
9. Drizzle with a little balsamic glaze.
10. Sprinkle with chives and basil. Enjoy.

### *Bruschetta with Cottage Cheese, Pears, and Hazelnuts*

A lovely, light way to start the day with a wholesome bruschetta that tempts the taste buds.

**Time:** 10 minutes

**Serving Size:** 1 | 2 | 4 servings

**Prep Time:** 5 minutes

**Cook Time:** 5 minutes

**Nutritional Facts/Info:**

Calories 156

Carbs 21.8 g

Fat 2.5 g

Protein 11.9 g

**Ingredients:**

- 1 sprouted multi-grain bread loaf (sliced, 2 slices each)
- 60 | 125 | 250 g low-fat cottage cheese
- ½ | 1 | 2 pears (cored, thinly sliced)
- 1 tbsp | 2 tbsp | ¼ cup roasted hazelnuts (chopped)
- Pure honey (to drizzle)
- 1 tbsp fresh thyme leaves (picked)

**Directions:**

1. Toast the bread until bruschetta is crispy as desired (grill if more than 4 pieces).
2. Spread bruschetta with a generous amount of cottage cheese.
3. Sprinkle with the chopped hazelnuts.
4. Fan with 3–4 slices of the pear.
5. Drizzle with a little honey and sprinkle with thyme leaves. Enjoy.

### *Spanish Omelet with Lemon Arugula*

Traditionally served hot, these omelets also make a good snack or brunch item. Popular as a tapas addition.

**Time:** 40 minutes

**Serving Size:** 1 | 2 | 4 servings

**Prep Time:** 10 minutes

**Cook Time:** 25 minutes

**Nutritional Facts/Info:**

Calories 262

Carbs 23.4 g

Fat 14.4 g

Protein 13 g

**Ingredients:**

- ½ | 1 | 2 medium potatoes (peeled, sliced thin)
- ½ | 1 | 2 tbsp extra virgin olive oil
- ¼ | ½ | 1 red onion (sliced thin)
- 2 | 4 | 6 free-range eggs
- ½ | 1 | 2 cups baby arugula rocket leaves
- 2 tbsp | ¼ |½ cup scallions (sliced)
- ¼ | ½ | 1 lemon (juiced, zested)
- ½ | 1 | 2 tbsp fresh flat leaf parsley (chopped, to serve)

**Directions:**

1. In a medium nonstick frying pan over medium-high, heat the oil.
2. Add the potatoes, then fry until tender and golden.
3. Add the onions and fry until translucent, then spread out with the potatoes evenly distributed, ready for the eggs.
4. Meanwhile, whisk the eggs with cracked black pepper to taste.
5. Pour the egg mixture into the frying pan over the potatoes and onion. Tilt the pan so the egg covers the base, then every so often so the raw egg mixture is distributed.

6. Cook until checking with an egg flip shows caramelization on the bottom, and the omelet is firm enough to flip.
7. Placing a dinner plate over the frying pan, gently tip the omelet onto the plate, then carefully slide it back into the frying pan to cook the other side.
8. The omelet is ready when it's browned underneath.
9. Mix the lemon juice, zest, scallions, and arugula leaves together in a small bowl.
10. Remove the omelet from the heat and cut into quarters.
11. Sprinkle with parsley.
12. Serve with the salad on the side. Enjoy.

### *Coffee Pikelets with Fruit*

The subtle hint of coffee in these pikelets adds a lovely flavor that pairs well with the fruit for a sophisticated breakfast.

**Time:** 25 minutes

**Serving Size:** 1 | 2 | 4 servings (makes 10)

**Prep Time:** 10 minutes

**Cook Time:** 15 minutes

**Nutritional Facts/Info:**

Calories 278

Carbs 42.1 g

Fat 6.4 g

Protein 13.9 g

**Ingredients:**

- ½ | 1 | 2 tbsp instant espresso coffee
- 50 | 100 | 200 g wholemeal self-raising flour
- ¼ | ½ | 1 tsp baking powder
- A pinch | ¼ | ½ tsp bicarbonate of soda

- ¼ | ½ | 1 tbsp caster sugar
- 1 free-range egg
- 50 | 100 | 200 g low-fat Greek yogurt (plus extra to serve)
- 50 | 100 | 200 ml unsweetened almond milk
- ¼ | ½ | 1 tbsp extra virgin olive oil
- Extra virgin olive oil cooking spray
- ¼ | ½ | 1 orange (peeled, segmented)
- 3 | 6 | 12 strawberries (hulled, halved)
- 3 | 6 | 12 black grapes
- Icing sugar (dusted through a sieve, to serve)
- ½ | 1 | 2 tsp lemon thyme leaves (picked, to serve)

**Directions:**

1. Mix the coffee with ½ | 1 | 2 tbsp of boiling water and set aside.
2. Sift the flour, baking powder, and bicarbonate of soda into a bowl.
3. Add the caster sugar and a pinch of salt.
4. In another bowl, whisk the egg, yogurt, milk, oil, and coffee until combined.
5. Add to dry ingredients and gently stir to combine. Set aside to form bubbles.
6. Heat a nonstick frying pan over medium heat and spray lightly with oil.
7. Working in batches, spoon 1 tbsp of batter into the pan for each pikelet.
8. Cook until bubbles form, then turn and cook for another minute or until brown underneath.
9. Cover and keep warm while repeating with remaining batter, spraying the pan with oil as required.
10. Arrange the pikelets in fanned stacks.
11. Top with fruit and a dollop of extra yogurt.
12. Lightly dust with icing sugar and sprinkle with thyme. Enjoy.

### *Halloumi Fritters with Corn, Broccoli, and Avocado*

The creamy dollops of yogurt make these crispy fritters so tasty and satisfying. They're still delectable cold and store well in airtight containers.

**Time:** 45 minutes

**Serving Size:** 1 | 2 | 4 servings (makes 8)

**Prep Time:** 15 minutes

**Cook Time:** 20 minutes

**Nutritional Facts/Info:**

Calories 336

Carbs 31.8 g

Fat 17.7 g

Protein 16.1 g

**Ingredients:**

- ⅛ | ¼ | ½ large head of broccoli (cut into large pieces including stem)
- 2 tbsp | ¼ | ½ cup wholemeal self-raising flour
- ¼ | ½ | 1 free-range egg
- 1 tbsp | 2 tbsp | ⅓ cup unsweetened almond milk
- 100 | 200 | 300 g can corn kernels (rinsed, drained) or 2 fresh cobs cooked and kernels removed
- 25 | 50 | 100 g halloumi (grated)
- ½ | 1 | 2 tbsp chopped fresh chives
- ¼ | ½ | 1 tsp finely grated lemon rind
- 1 tbsp | 2 tbsp | ¼ cup extra virgin olive oil
- ¼ | ½ | 1 cup baby spinach leaves (to serve)
- ¼ | ½ | 1 avocado (skinned, stoned, and sliced, to serve)
- 3 | 6 | 12 grape tomatoes (halved, to serve)
- ½ cup spring onions (sliced finely)
- ½ cup low-fat Greek yogurt (to serve)
- ¼ cup mixed seeds (to serve)

## Directions:

1. Add broccoli pieces to a food processor or blender. Pulse, scraping down the side occasionally until finely chopped.
2. In a large bowl, add the self-raising flour and egg, then slowly pour in the milk, whisking until the mixture is smooth.
3. Add the broccoli, corn, halloumi, chives, and lemon rind to the flour mixture, then season. Using a wooden spoon, stir to combine.
4. In a large nonstick frying pan, heat ¼ | ½ | 1 tbsp oil over medium heat.
5. Cooking in batches to make 2 | 4 | 8 fritters, spoon ¼ cups of the fritter mixture into the pan using an egg flip to flatten slightly.
6. Cook the fritters for 2 minutes or until golden.
7. Carefully turn with an egg flip, then cook further 2 minutes until golden and cooked through.
8. Transfer to a plate lined with paper towel or keep warm in a low oven.
9. Repeat the process with the remaining oil and mixture to finish the fritters.
10. Arrange the fritters on a serving platter or plates, scattering the edges with spinach and tomatoes.
11. Fan the avocado on top of each fritter, then dollop with yogurt.
12. Sprinkle with spring onions and mixed seeds. Enjoy.

### *Chargrilled Honey Plums*

A sweet start to the day that's low in fat and succulent.

**Time:** 35 minutes

**Serving Size:** 1 | 2 | 4 servings

**Prep Time:** 10 minutes

**Cook Time:** 15 minutes

**Nutritional Facts/Info:**

Calories 176

Carbs 31.6 g

Fat 3.3 g

Protein 8.7 g

**Ingredients:**

- 2 | 4 | 8 medium plums (halved, stoned)
- Extra virgin olive oil cooking spray
- ¼ | ½ | 1 tsp pure honey, plus extra to drizzle
- ¼ | ½ | 1 cup toasted whole grain muesli with nuts
- ⅜ | ¾ | 1½ cups low-fat Greek yogurt
- 2 | 4 | 8 basil leaves (chopped finely)
- A pinch | ¼ | ½ tsp ground cinnamon
- 1 | 2 | 4 sprigs basil (to serve)

**Directions:**

1. Set the oven to 350 °F/180 °C, then heat a chargrill pan over high heat.
2. Spray the cut side of the fruit with oil, then cook cut side down for 1–2 minutes until charred with lines. Place upright in an ovenproof dish.
3. Drizzle the plums with honey, then sprinkle with most of the muesli.
4. Cook in the oven for 10 minutes until the plums are tender.
5. In a small bowl, mix the yogurt with cinnamon, chopped basil, and 1 tsp honey. Chill.
6. When the plums are cooked, remove from the oven and lay out on a serving platter or plates.
7. Top plums with dollops of yogurt, then sprinkle with remaining muesli.
8. Scatter the basil around the plums and serve.

### *Vegetarian Frittata*

A scrumptious frittata that everyone will simply enjoy eating.

**Time:** 1 hour

**Serving Size:** 1 | 2 | 4 servings

**Prep Time:** 15 minutes

**Cook Time:** 35 minutes

**Nutritional Facts/Info:**

Calories 262

Carbs 16 g

Fat 14.7 g

Protein 18.1 g

**Ingredients:**

- ⅜ | ¾ | 1½ tbsp extra virgin olive oil
- ½ | 1 | 2 zucchinis (sliced thinly)
- 2 tbsp | ¼ | ½ cup button mushrooms (sliced thinly)
- ½ | 1 | 2 garlic cloves (crushed)
- A pinch | ¼ | ½ tsp dried chili flakes
- 25 | 50 | 100 g kale (chopped)
- ¼ | ½ | 1 cup frozen peas
- ½ cup cherry tomatoes (halved)
- 2 | 4 | 8 free-range eggs
- ½ | 1 | 2 tbsp unsweetened almond milk
- 25 | 45 | 85 g fat-free ricotta
- 1 | 2 | 4 slices whole grain sourdough bread
- ¼ | ½ | 1 lemon (wedged, to serve)
- ¼ | ½ | 1 tbsp fresh rosemary (picked, to serve)

**Directions:**

1. Whisk the eggs and milk together in a large jug. Season and set aside.

2. In a large, ovenproof nonstick frying pan over medium-high, heat half the olive oil.

3. Add the zucchini and cook, turning for 2–3 minutes or until golden. Transfer to a plate lined with paper towel.

4. Add the garlic, chili, and remaining oil, then cook, stirring for 1 minute or until aromatic.

5. Add the mushrooms and cook, stirring for 2–3 minutes until starting to soften.

6. Add the kale and peas, then cook until the kale wilts.

7. Add the cherry tomatoes.

8. Return the zucchini to the pan, then lay out the vegetables evenly over the base.

9. Pour the egg mixture evenly over the vegetables, then dollop here and there with the ricotta.

10. Reduce heat to low, then cover and cook for 15 minutes or until the egg mixture almost sets. (A little wobble is fine.)

11. Set broiler or grill to high.

12. Place the frittata under the grill and cook for 5 minutes or until golden, set, and puffed.

13. Remove from the grill, sprinkle with fresh rosemary, and set aside for 5 minutes before cutting into 4 wedges.

14. Toast the whole grain bread and serve the frittata with lemon wedges.


SMOOTHIES

Although Mediterraneans aren't in the habit of drinking smoothies, we can use the principles of the diet to create healthy smoothie options for people in industrialized countries.

What a delicious, nutritious way to start the day—especially if you're short on time. If you don't have fresh fruit, use frozen varieties. For busy people, it's easy to make smoothies up to 2 days in advance and keep them in the fridge. Make smoothie batches ahead of time, then freeze them in airtight containers or thick plastic bags. Simply thaw overnight, and always give the smoothie a good shake before drinking.

### Mango, Yogurt, and Mint Smoothie

A chilling, refreshing smoothie to start the day off with a smile.

**Time:** 5 minutes

**Serving Size:** 1 | 2 | 4 servings

**Prep Time:** 5 minutes

**Nutritional Facts/Info:**

Calories 245

Carbs 39.7 g

Fat 6.31 g

Protein 9 g

**Ingredients:**

- ½ | 1 | 2 cups low-fat Greek yogurt
- 125 | 250 | 500 g fresh mango chunks or frozen (thawed)
- ¼ | ½ | 1 cup skim, soy, or unsweetened almond milk
- ½ | 1 | 2 tbsp pure honey
- ¼ | ½ | 1 tsp cinnamon
- 1¼ tbsp | 2½ tbsp | ⅓ cup toasted coconut flakes
- 4 sprigs fresh mint

**Directions:**

1. Add yogurt, mango, milk, honey, and cinnamon to a blender, then blend for 20 seconds until smooth.
2. Serve in chilled glasses topped with coconut flakes and mint sprigs.

### Berry Bran Smoothie

With the addition of All-Bran cereal, this is a deceptively filling smoothie that ticks all the boxes for taste and nutrition.

**Time:** 10 minutes

**Serving Size:** 1 | 2 | 4 servings

**Prep Time:** 5 minutes

**Nutritional Facts/Info:**

Calories 78

Carbs 18.7 g

Fat 0.4 g

Protein 3.3 g

**Ingredients:**

- 2 tbsp | ¼ | 1/2 cup mixed berries like blueberries, strawberries, and blackberries
- ¼ | ½ | 1 banana (peeled, sliced)
- 2 tbsp | ¼ | ½ cup All-Bran cereal (or similar)
- 2 tbsp | ¼ | ½ cup low-fat Greek yogurt
- 1 | 2 | 4 sprigs fresh mint

**Directions:**

1. Place half the All-Bran, half the banana, a handful of the berries, and yogurt into a blender.
2. Blend until creamy and smooth.
3. Pour into small bowls.
4. Sprinkle remaining All-Bran, berries, and banana on top.
5. Garnish with a sprig of mint and serve.

### Pick-Me-Up Smoothie

An energy-boosting, low-calorie smoothie that promotes healthy skin.

**Time:** 10 minutes

**Serving Size:** 1 | 2 | 4 servings

**Prep Time:** 10 minutes

**Nutritional Facts/Info:**

Calories 191

Carbs 27 g

Fat 10.4 g

Protein 3 g

**Ingredients:**

- ¼ | ½ | 1 small lemon (quartered with skin on)
- ¼ | ½ | 1 large green apple (peeled, cored, and quartered)
- ¼ | ½ | 1 x 2 in/5 cm piece of fresh ginger root (peeled if desired)
- ½ | 1 | 2 cups coconut water, water, or unsweetened almond milk
- ¼ | ½ | 1 banana (peeled)
- ¼ | ½ | 1 avocado (peeled, stoned)
- ¼ | ½ | 1 cucumber (chopped)
- ¼ | ½ | 1 tbsp pure honey
- A pinch of sea salt
- ½ cup of ice
- ¼ | ½ | 1 tsp fresh thyme leaves (plus ¼ | ½ | 1 tsp extra, to serve)
- 1 small lime (sliced, to serve)

**Directions:**

1. In a blender, add the lemon, apple, ginger, ½ cup coconut water, and some ice, then blend.
2. Add the rest of the smoothie ingredients and blend again until smooth.

3. Serve into glasses, then sprinkle with the remaining thyme leaves.

4. Slice halfway through each lime slice, then set on the top side of the glasses. Enjoy.

## *Fruity Date Smoothie*

Cacao is high in protein, magnesium, iron, and fiber and a healthier choice than cocoa. It makes a lovely addition to this lip-smacking smoothie.

**Time:** 5 minutes

**Serving Size:** 1 | 2 | 4 servings

**Prep Time:** 5 minutes

**Nutritional Facts/Info:**

Calories 226

Carbs 34 g

Fat 10.3 g

Protein 5.8 g

**Ingredients:**

- 2 | 4 | 8 pitted medjool dates
- ½ | 1 | 2 large bananas (peeled, quartered)
- ¼ | ½ | 1 red apple (peeled, cored)
- 2 tbsp | ¼ | ½ cup raw cashews
- 1½ tsp | ¾ | 1½ tbsp cacao powder
- 1½ tsp | ¾ | 1½ cups unsweetened almond milk
- 1½ tsp | ½ | 1 tbsp sesame seeds (to serve)

**Directions:**

1. Place all the ingredients except the sesame seeds into a blender.

2. Blend until creamy and smooth.
3. Pour into glasses.
4. Sprinkle with sesame seeds and serve.

### Energy Booster Smoothie

The perfect smoothie for active people that use up a lot of energy. Athletes could add a tablespoon of protein powder for an extra boost.

**Time:** 5 minutes

**Serving Size:** 1 | 2 | 4 servings

**Prep Time:** 5 minutes

**Nutritional Facts/Info:**

Calories 330

Carbs 34.8 g

Fat 21 g

Protein 6.7 g

**Ingredients:**

- ½ | 1 | 2 ripe bananas (peeled)
- ½ | 1 | 2 avocados (stoned, peeled)
- 40 | 75 | 150 g spinach
- ¼ | ½ | 1 cucumber (chopped)
- ¼ | ½ | 1 celery stick (chopped)
- 6 tbsp | ¾ | 1½ cups unsweetened almond milk
- 1 tsp | ¾ | 1½ tbsp pure honey
- ¼ | ½ | 1 tsp cinnamon
- ¼ | ½ | 1 tbsp unsweetened coconut flakes (to serve)
- ¼ | ½ | 1 tbsp mixed seeds like linseed, chia, and pepitas (to serve)
- 2 tbsp | ¼ | ½ tbsp chopped raw peanuts (to serve)

**Directions:**

1. Process all ingredients in a blender, then pour into glasses.
2. Sprinkle with the mixed seeds, chopped peanuts, and coconut flakes. Enjoy.

### *Sunflower Smoothie*

A terrific low-calorie smoothie that will give you enough energy to tackle the day ahead.

**Time:** 5 minutes

**Serving Size:** 1 | 2 | 4 servings

**Prep Time:** 5 minutes

**Nutritional Facts/Info:**

Calories 131

Carbs 19.4 g

Fat 5.1 g

Protein 2.7 g

**Ingredients:**

- ⅙ | ⅓ | ⅔ Lebanese cucumber (quartered)
- ¼ | ½ | 1 green apple (cored, quartered)
- ¼ | ½ | 1 tbsp parsley
- ⅓ | ⅔ | 1⅓ tbsp sunflower seeds
- ⅓ | ⅔ | 1⅓ kale leaves (chopped)
- ⅔ | 1⅓ | 2⅔ cups unsweetened almond milk
- ⅔ | 1⅓ | 2⅔ tsp pure honey

**Directions:**

1. Place all the ingredients into a blender, then blend until smooth.
2. Pour into tall glasses.

### *Summer Fun Smoothie Bowl*

You can have a bit of fun with smoothies by decorating them with fruit, nuts, seeds, and cereal—especially if you have young children. We're going to make this one look like a fish in the sea.

**Time:** 10 minutes

**Serving Size:** 1 | 2 | 4 servings

**Prep Time:** 10 minutes

**Nutritional Facts/Info:**

Calories 265

Carbs 55.6 g

Fat 3.5 g

Protein 5.3 g

**Ingredients:**

- 112 | 225 | 450 g frozen blueberries
- ¼ | ½ | 1 banana (peeled, chopped)
- ¼ | ½ | 1 cucumber (chopped)
- ½ | 1 | 2 kiwi fruit (sliced)
- ¼ | ½ | 1 tsp cinnamon
- 3 tbsp | 6 tbsp | ¾ cup whole grain rolled oats
- ¾ | 1½ | 3 cups unsweetened almond milk
- 1½ tbsp | 2½ tbsp |⅓ cup fruit muesli
- ¼ | ½ | 1 orange (sliced)

**Directions:**

1. Add 100 | 200 | 400 g blueberries, banana, cucumber, cinnamon, oats, and milk to a blender, then blend until smooth.
2. Cut the triangular fish fin and tail shapes from the sliced kiwifruit. Set aside.

3. Divide the smoothie mix into shallow bowls, then scatter muesli around a third of the bottom curved edge to form the sandy seafloor.

4. Arrange one orange slice above the sand for the fish, then add kiwifruit fish fins and a tail.

5. Use the leftover blueberries for the eye and fish bubbles coming up out of the mouth. Serve and enjoy!

### *Lean Green Smoothie*

If you want a good head start to slimming, drink this low-calorie, low-fat smoothie for a quick breakfast or snack several times a week.

**Time:** 5 minutes

**Serving Size:** 1 | 2 | 4 servings

**Prep Time:** 5 minutes

**Nutritional Facts/Info:**

Calories 101

Carbs 20.4 g

Fat 2 g

Protein 2.7 g

**Ingredients:**

- ¼ | ½ | 1 green apple (cored, chopped)
- ¼ | ½ | 1 cucumber
- ¼ | ½ | 1 piece ginger root 1 in/2½ cm
- ½ | 1 | 2 kiwi fruit (peeled, halved)
- ¼ | ½ | 1 large celery stick 12 in/30 cm
- ¼ | ½ | 1 cup unsweetened apple juice
- ¼ | ½ | 1 cup baby spinach leaves
- ⅛ | ¼ | ½ lemon
- 1¼ tbsp | 2½ tbsp | ⅓ cup mint leaves
- ½ | 1 | 2 tsp pepita seeds (to serve)

## Directions:

1. Process all ingredients in a blender, then pour over ice.
2. Sprinkle with the pepitas and serve.

### *Fruit and Oats Smoothie*

This smoothie tastes great and is a filling drink that will keep you going for several hours.

**Time:** 5 minutes

**Serving Size:** 1 | 2 | 4 servings

**Prep Time:** 5 minutes

**Nutritional Facts/Info:**

Calories 173

Carbs 31.3 g

Fat 2.2 g

Protein 8.5 g

**Ingredients:**

- ¼ | ½ | 1 cup strawberries (hulled)
- ½ | 1 | 2 bananas (peeled)
- ¼ | ½ | 1 tsp cinnamon
- 2 tbsp | ¼ | ½ cup whole grain rolled oats
- ¼ | ½ | 1 cup unsweetened almond milk
- ¼ | ½ | 1 cup low-fat Greek yogurt
- 1 tbsp | 2 tbsp | ¼ cup muesli fruit and with nuts (to serve)

**Directions:**

1. Process all ingredients in a blender, then pour into glasses.
2. Sprinkle with a little muesli and serve.

### Choc Beet Berry Smoothie

A nourishing, low-fat smoothie packed full of flavor to tempt your tastebuds.

**Time:** 5 minutes

**Serving Size:** 1 | 2 | 4 servings

**Prep Time:** 5 minutes

**Nutritional Facts/Info:**

Calories 219

Carbs 37.1 g

Fat 6.5 g

Protein 9.9 g

**Ingredients:**

- ½ | 1 | 2 bananas (peeled)
- 40 | 75 | 150 g fresh beetroot (peeled, chopped)
- ¼ | ½ | 1 cup frozen raspberries
- ½ | 1 | 2 cups unsweetened almond milk
- 50 | 100 | 200 g low-fat Greek yogurt
- ¼ | ½ | 1 cup whole grain rolled oats
- ¼ | ½ | 1 tbsp chia seeds
- ¼ | ½ | 1 tbsp tahini
- ¼ | ½ | 1 tbsp cacao powder (plus extra to serve)

**Directions:**

1. Process all ingredients in a blender with a few ice cubes until smooth, then pour into tall glasses.
2. Sprinkle with the extra cacao and serve.

# CHAPTER 6
## MAIN MEAL RECIPES

SOUP

### *Roast Kumara Soup with Kale, Cashews, and Feta*

A lovely light meal with a delicious depth of flavor that will delight your dinner companions.

**Time:** 1 hour 10 minutes

**Serving Size:** 1 | 2 | 4 servings

**Prep Time:** 30 minutes

**Cook Time:** 40 minutes

**Nutritional Facts/Info:**

Calories 369

Carbs 51.4 g

Fat 13.1 g

Protein 13 g

## Ingredients:

- 200 | 400 | 800 g medium golden sweet potatoes (halved lengthwise)
- ¼ | ½ | 1 brown onion (unskinned)
- ¾ | 1½ | 3 cloves garlic (unskinned)
- Extra virgin olive oil cooking spray
- 250 ml | 500 ml | 1 l salt-reduced vegetable stock
- 100 | 200 | 400 g cannellini beans (rinsed, drained)
- ¼ | ½ | 1 cup skim, soy, or almond milk
- 1 tbsp | 2 tbsp | ¼ cup raw cashews (coarsely chopped)
- ¼ | ½ | 1 cup fresh kale (stalks finely chopped, leaves chopped)
- ½ | 1 | 2 tbsp extra virgin olive oil
- 1 tbsp | 2 tbsp | ¼ bunch coriander sprigs (to serve)
- A pinch | a pinch |¼ tsp dried chili flakes (to serve)
- ¼ | ½ | 1 wholemeal pita bread rounds (quartered, to serve)

## Directions:

1. Set oven to 450 °F/220 °C or 400 °F/200 °C, fan forced, and line a baking tray with parchment paper.
2. Place sweet potato cut side down on the tray with the onion and garlic. Spray with olive oil.
3. Roast for 30 minutes or until potato is tender when pierced with a fork. Set aside for 10 minutes to cool slightly.
4. In the meantime, reduce the oven to 400 °F/200 °C or 350 °F/180 °C, fan forced.
5. In a bowl, mix together the cashews, kale, sumac, and oil, ensuring the kale leaves are coated. Add to the oven tray.
6. Place the bread on the same tray, then bake for 10 minutes or until the bread browns and the kale is crispy.
7. Scoop the sweet potato flesh out of the potatoes, then remove and discard skins from the garlic and onion.
8. Add the sweet potato, onion, and garlic flesh to a food processor with the vegetable stock, cannellini beans, and half the milk. Process until smooth.

9. Ladle soup among bowls and drizzle with remaining milk. Crack with pepper.
10. Top with the kale mixture, then sprinkle with chili flakes, crumbled feta, and coriander.
11. Serve with warm pita bread.

### *Pesto Chicken Soup with Chickpeas*

A hearty, satisfying soup to enjoy on a winter night with delicious basil overtones.

**Time:** 40 minutes

**Serving Size:** 1 | 2 | 4 servings

**Prep Time:** 15 minutes

**Cook Time:** 25 minutes

**Nutritional Facts/Info:**

Calories 389

Carbs 46.7 g

Fat 19.7 g

Protein 20.8 g

**Ingredients:**

- Extra virgin olive oil cooking spray
- ¼ | ½ | 1 brown onion (chopped finely)
- ½ | 1 | 2 garlic cloves (crushed)
- ¼ | ½ | 1 carrot (peeled, chopped)
- ¼ | ½ | 1 stick celery (chopped)
- 100 | 200 | 400 g diced tomatoes
- 1 | 2 | 4 cups chicken stock
- 100 | 200 | 400 g chicken breast fillets (trimmed, chopped into bite-size pieces)
- 100 | 200 | 400 g chickpeas (rinsed, drained)

- 25 | 50 | 100 g green beans (ends trimmed, cut into thirds)
- ¼ | ½ | 1 tbsp basil pesto
- 1 | 2 | 4 crusty wholegrain bread rolls (to serve)

## Directions:

1. Spray a large saucepan with oil and heat to medium.
2. Add the onion and garlic, then cook, stirring occasionally until onion softens.
3. Add the carrot and celery, then cook for 5 minutes.
4. Add the tomatoes and stock to the pan, increasing heat to medium-high.
5. Bring to a boil, then add the chopped chicken. Reduce heat to medium.
6. Simmer uncovered for 10 minutes or until chicken is just cooked through.
7. Add the chickpeas and beans, then cook for 5 minutes.
8. Add the basil pesto and season.
9. Ladle into bowls, then serve with the crusty bread rolls.

### *Tomato Vegetable Soup with Baby Bocconcini*

A tasty, healthy soup topped with little balls of melting mozzarella.

**Time:** 1 hour 5 minutes

**Serving Size:** 1 | 2 | 4 servings

**Prep Time:** 25 minutes

**Cook Time:** 40 minutes

**Nutritional Facts/Info:**

Calories 332

Carbs 42.4 g

Fat 13.8 g

Protein 14.1 g

## Ingredients:

- 185 | 375 | 750 g Roma tomatoes (halved)
- Caster sugar (to sprinkle)
- Italian mixed dried herbs (to sprinkle)
- Extra virgin olive oil (to drizzle)
- ¼ | ½ | 1 tbsp extra virgin olive oil
- ½ | 1 | 2 brown onions (diced)
- ½ | 1 | 2 medium-sized carrots (diced)
- ½ | 1 | 2 celery stalks (diced)
- ¾ | 1½ | 3 garlic cloves (finely chopped)
- 100 | 200 | 400 g tin of diced tomatoes
- 185 | 375 | 750 g vegetable stock
- 1 | 2 | 4 sprigs fresh basil, plus extra leaves to serve
- ¼ | ½ | 1 tbsp fresh rosemary (leaves chopped)
- 55 | 110 | 220 g baby bocconcini
- 1 | 2 | 4 slices whole grain bread

## Directions:

1. Set the oven to 320 °F/160 °C and line a baking tray with parchment paper.
2. Place Roma tomatoes cut side up on a baking tray. Sprinkle with pinches of sugar and mixed herbs. Drizzle with oil and season.
3. Roast for 30 minutes until soft.
4. Meanwhile, in a large saucepan, heat the oil over medium heat.
5. Cook onion, carrot, celery, and garlic stirring for 4–5 minutes until soft.
6. Add tinned tomatoes, basil, vegetable stock, roasted Roma tomatoes, and roasting juice.
7. Bring to a boil, then reduce heat to low and simmer, stirring occasionally for 30 minutes.
8. Allow the mixture to cool slightly, then carefully blend the soup in the saucepan with a stick blender.
9. To serve, you may need to reheat gently first.

10. Pour the soup into bowls, then drop the desired amount of bocconcini into the bowls.
11. Season and garnish with extra basil leaves.
12. Serve with whole grain bread.

### *Broccolini Soup with Orzo*

A broccoli soup just like Nonna used to make, but with extra goodies on top!

**Time:** 30 minutes

**Serving Size:** 1 | 2 | 4 servings

**Prep Time:** 10 minutes

**Cook Time:** 15 minutes

**Nutritional Facts/Info:**

Calories 249

Carbs 30.7 g

Fat 11.2 g

Protein 11.5 g

**Ingredients:**

- ¼ | ½ | 1 tbsp extra virgin olive oil
- ¼ | ½ | 1 onion (diced)
- 1 | 2 | 4 cloves garlic (crushed)
- 115 | 225 | 450 g broccolini (chopped)
- 1 | 2 | 4 cups salt-reduced vegetable stock
- A pinch | ⅛ | ¼ tsp nutmeg
- 3 tbsp | ⅜ | ¾ cup orzo or risoni
- ¼ | ½ | 1 tbsp fresh thyme leaves (picked, plus extra to serve)
- 2 tbsp | ¼ | ½ cup shaved parmigiano reggiano parmesan (to serve)
- Extra virgin olive oil spray

- 25 | 50 | 100 g speck (skin removed, diced)
- 1 | 2 | 4 slices crusty wholemeal bread

**Directions:**

1. In a large saucepan over medium heat, add the oil.
2. Add the onion and garlic to the pan, then sauté until soft.
3. Add the orzo and sauté for a minute.
4. Add the stock, broccolini, nutmeg, and thyme.
5. Bring to a boil, reduce heat, and simmer for 10 minutes, stirring occasionally to ensure pasta doesn't stick.
6. Meanwhile, in a small nonstick frying pan on medium-high, spray with cooking oil, then add the speck. Cook, shaking the pan until caramelized and crispy.
7. Ladle the soup into bowls, then sprinkle with parmesan and thyme.
8. Sprinkle the speck around the middle of each bowl, then serve with crusty bread.

### *Sicilian Potato and Beef Soup*

A delicious soup that warms any winter night.

**Time:** 1 hour

**Serving Size:** 1 | 2 | 4 servings

**Prep Time:** 15 minutes

**Cook Time:** 45 minutes

**Nutritional Facts/Info:**

Calories 305

Carbs 10 g

Fat 13.9 g

Protein 33.9 g

## Ingredient :

- 2 tbsp | ¼ | ½ cup extra virgin olive oil
- ¼ | ½ | 1 onion (diced)
- 100 | 200 | 400 g potatoes (diced)
- 125 | 250 | 500 g chuck steak (trimmed, cut into 1 in/2½ cm cubes)
- 2 tbsp | ¼ | ½ cup frozen peas
- 250 ml | 500 ml | 1 l hot water
- ¼ | ½ | 1 tbsp flat leaf parsley (picked)

## Directions:

1. In a large saucepan over medium heat, add ½ | 1 | 2 tbsp oil and heat.
2. Fry for 2 minutes until the onions are translucent. Transfer to a bowl and set aside.
3. Add ¼ | ½ | 1 tbsp oil to the pan and, working in batches, sauté the potato for 4 minutes.
4. Turn and cook another 4 minutes until crisp, adding more oil if required.
5. Transfer to the bowl with the onion.
6. Reheat the pan to high and add the beef, sautéing for ~7 minutes until sealed all over.
7. Add hot water to cover the beef, then season with salt and plenty of black pepper.
8. Reduce heat to low and simmer for 30 minutes until tender.
9. Add the onion and potato to the saucepan, then simmer for 10 minutes until the potato is tender.
10. Add the peas during the last 5 minutes of cooking.
11. Ladle into bowls and sprinkle with parsley. Enjoy.

### *Lamb and Veggie Soup with Barley*

There's nothing like a hearty veggie soup with barley to satisfy and nourish the soul.

**Time:** 55 minutes

**Serving Size:** 1 | 2 | 4 servings

**Prep Time:** 10 minutes

**Cook Time:** 40 minutes

**Nutritional Facts/Info:**

Calories 350

Carbs 43.8 g

Fat 10.4 g

Protein 22.5 g

**Ingredients:**

- ¼ | ½ | 1 tbsp extra virgin olive oil
- 65 | 125 | 250 g lamb leg steaks (cut into small cubes, seasoned)
- ½ | 1 | 2 sticks celery (sliced)
- ¼ | ½ | 1 onion (diced)
- 185 | 375 | 750 g root vegetables like carrots, parsnip, turnip (peeled, diced)
- 2 tbsp | ¼ | ½ cup pearl barley (rinsed)
- 1 | 2 | 4 cups beef stock
- ½ | 1 | 2 tsp Worcestershire sauce
- 1 | 2 | 4 thyme sprigs
- 2 tbsp | ¼ |½ cup frozen peas
- 1 tbsp | 2 tbsp | ¼ cup parsley (chopped)
- 1 | 2 | 4 slices crusty whole grain bread (to serve)

**Directions:**

1. In a large saucepan over medium-high heat, add the lamb and cook for 5 minutes sealing all sides.
2. Add the onion and celery, then cook for 3 minutes.
3. Stir in vegetables, barley, stock, sauce, and thyme.

4. Bring to a boil, then reduce heat to low. Cover and simmer for 30 minutes until barley is tender.
5. Remove thyme stems and stir in parsley and peas.
6. Ladle into soup bowls and sprinkle with basil.
7. Serve with bread.

### *Creamy Pea and Feta Soup with Pistachios*

If you like pea soup, then you'll love this quick version using frozen peas.

**Time:** 35 minutes

**Serving Size:** 1 | 2 | 4 servings

**Prep Time:** 10 minutes

**Cook Time:** 15 minutes

**Nutritional Facts/Info:**

Calories 239

Carbs 25.7 g

Fat 11.2 g

Protein 10.8 g

**Ingredients:**

- ¼ | ½ | 1 tbsp extra virgin olive oil
- ¼ | ½ | 1 onion (chopped)
- ¼ | ½ | 1 tsp minced garlic
- ¼ | ½ | 1 washed potato (diced)
- ½ | 1 | 2 cups salt-reduced chicken stock
- ⅜ | ¾ | 1½ cups unsweetened almond milk
- ¾ | 1½ | 3 cups frozen baby peas
- ⅛| ¼ | ½ tbsp fresh rosemary (finely chopped)
- ½ | 1 | 2 tsp thyme leaves (picked)
- 25 | 50 | 100 g feta (crumbled)

- 1 tbsp | 2 tbsp | ¼ cup shelled pistachio nuts (chopped)
- Snow pea sprouts (to serve)

**Directions:**

1. In a large saucepan over medium heat, add oil, onion, and garlic. Cook for 5 minutes until onion is translucent.
2. Add potatoes and cook for a further 5 minutes.
3. Add stock, milk, peas, rosemary, and thyme, then stir.
4. Reduce heat and simmer for 5 minutes until heated through.
5. With a stick blender, carefully blend mixture until smooth.
6. Ladle into soup bowls.
7. Sprinkle with crumbled feta and pistachios.
8. Top with snow pea tendrils and serve.

### *Bean Soup with Parsley Oil*

The aroma of parsley precedes this delicious soup with a crispy, spicy chorizo hit that makes the mouth water.

**Time:** 55 minutes

**Serving Size:** 1 | 2 | 4 servings

**Prep Time:** 15 minutes

**Cook Time:** 30 minutes

## Nutritional Facts/Info:

Calories 299

Carbs 25.8 g

Fat 20 g

Protein 8.5 g

## Ingredients:

- ¼ | ½ | 1 tbsp extra virgin olive oil
- ¼ | ½ | 1 onion (chopped)
- ½ | 1 | 2 garlic cloves (crushed)
- 50 | 100 | 200 g sweet potato (peeled, diced)
- 1 | 2 | 4 cups salt-reduced chicken stock
- 100 | 200 | 400 g diced tomatoes
- ¼ | ½ | 1 cup flat-leaf parsley (picked)
- 1 tbsp | 2 tbsp | ¼ cup extra virgin olive oil
- 100 | 200 | 400 g can red kidney beans (rinsed, drained)
- ¼ | ½ | 1 chorizo (sliced)
- 1 | 2 | 4 sprigs oregano leaves (to serve)

## Directions:

1. In a large saucepan over medium-low, heat the oil.
2. Add onion and cook for 5 minutes until soft.
3. Add garlic and sweet potato, then cook for 2 minutes.
4. Pour in stock and tomatoes, then simmer for 15 minutes until potato is tender.
5. Meanwhile, boil water in a kettle, then add some to a jug.
6. Add parsley to the jug for 30 seconds to blanch until bright green. Drain, then refresh in cold water and drain again.
7. Add parsley to a food processor and puree.
8. Add oil and process until combined. Set aside.
9. With a stick blender, carefully puree the soup in the pot.
10. Add kidney beans and stir, keeping warm over low heat.

11. In a small, nonstick frying pan on high heat, add the chorizo slices and sauté until crisp. Remove onto a paper towel.
12. Ladle soup into soup bowls.
13. Top with chorizo and drizzle with parsley oil.
14. Sprinkle with oregano and serve.

### Green Leek and Potato Soup with Paprika Crisps

A healthy version of this classic soup is made memorable with the crispy paprika potato skins.

**Time:** 45 minutes

**Serving Size:** 1 | 2 | 4 servings

**Prep Time:** 10 minutes

**Cook Time:** 20 minutes

**Nutritional Facts/Info:**

Calories 275

Carbs 43.8 g

Fat 8.5 g

Protein 8 g

**Ingredients:**

- 100 | 200 | 400 g washed white potatoes (peeled, skins reserved, and diced into ¾ in/2 cm pieces)
- Paprika (to sprinkle)
- 1 tbsp | 2 tbsp | ¼ cup extra virgin olive oil
- ½ | 1 | 2 leeks (trimmed, sliced thinly)
- ¼ | ½ | 1 onion (finely diced)
- ¼ | ½ | 1 tbsp fresh thyme leaves (picked)
- 1 | 2 | 4 cloves garlic (crushed)
- ½ | 1 | 2 cups salt-reduced vegetable stock
- 30 | 60 | 120 g baby spinach leaves

- 1 tbsp | 2 tbsp | ⅓ cup low-fat Greek yogurt
- ¼ | ½ | 1 tbsp fresh sage leaves (picked, torn)
- 1 | 2 | 4 slices wholemeal whole grain bread (to serve)

## Directions:

1. Spread the potato skins out on paper towel and pat dry. Sprinkle with paprika.
2. In a large saucepan over medium-high, heat the oil.
3. Cook potato skins for 2 minutes or until golden and crisp. Transfer to a plate lined with paper towel, then set aside.
4. Heat remaining oil in the pan, then add leek, onion, thyme, garlic, and chopped potatoes.
5. Sauté for 4 minutes or until onion and leek are soft.
6. Add stock plus 2 cups water, then bring to a boil.
7. Reduce heat to medium and simmer uncovered for 12 minutes or until potato is tender.
8. Stir in spinach.
9. Using a stick blender, carefully puree the soup until smooth. Season.
10. Toast the bread.
11. Divide among soup bowls, dollop with yogurt, and top with potato skins.
12. Sprinkle with sage and cracked pepper.
13. Serve with toasted bread. Enjoy.

### *Parsnip Soup with Olives and Prosciutto Crisps*

Tasty and satisfying, this low-calorie soup shines with creamy yogurt and crunchy prosciutto crisps.

**Time:** 45 minutes

**Serving Size:** 1 | 2 | 4 servings

**Prep Time:** 10 minutes

**Cook Time:** 30 minutes

**Nutritional Facts/Info:**

Calories 213

Carbs 31.9 g

Fat 8.8 g

Protein 4.9 g

**Ingredients:**

- ¼ | ½ | 1 tbsp extra virgin olive oil
- ¼ | ½ | 1 bay leaf
- ¼ | ½ | 1 green apple (peeled, cored, and diced)
- ¼ | ½ | 1 onion (chopped)
- 125 | 250 | 500 g parsnips (peeled, diced)
- 1 | 2 | 4 cups salt-reduced chicken stock
- 1 tbsp | 2 tbsp | ¼ cup pitted green olives (halved)
- ¾ | 1½ | 3 slices prosciutto
- 1 | 2 | 4 tbsp low-fat Greek yogurt (to serve)
- ¼ | ½ | 1 tbsp chives (snipped, to serve)

**Directions:**

1. In a large saucepan over medium heat, add the oil and sauté the onion, parsnip, and apple for 5 minutes until the onion softens.
2. Add the stock, bay leaf, and bring to a boil. Reduce heat to low and cook for 20 minutes until parsnip is very tender. Turn off heat.
3. Remove and discard bay leaf.
4. Using a stick blender, carefully puree the soup until smooth.
5. Add the olives and season with pepper.
6. Meanwhile, in a medium nonstick frying pan over medium-high heat, cook the prosciutto until crisp.
7. Transfer to a paper towel. Leave a few minutes to cool, then snap to form crispy bits.
8. Ladle soup into bowls.

9. Dollop with yogurt.
10. Sprinkle with prosciutto crisps and chives. Enjoy.

### *Greek Chicken Soup with Lemon*

A comfort soup to the Greeks and anyone else who tastes it!

**Time:** 45 minutes

**Serving Size:** 1 | 2 | 4 servings

**Prep Time:** 5 minutes

**Cook Time:** 25 minutes

**Nutritional Facts/Info:**

Calories 197

Carbs 10 g

Fat 5.3 g

Protein 28.5 g

**Ingredients:**

- 100 | 200 | 400 g chicken breast fillets
- 1 | 2 | 4 cups salt-reduced chicken stock
- 1¼ tbsp | 2½ tbsp | ⅓ cup arborio rice
- ¼ | ½ | 1 cup dill leaves (picked, stems finely chopped to use separately)
- ½ | 1 | 2 lemons (juiced, zested)
- 1 | 1 | 2 free-range eggs
- Extra virgin olive oil (to serve)
- 1 | 2 | 4 fresh basil leaves (to serve)

**Directions:**

1. In a large saucepan over medium-high heat, add chicken, stock, rice, dill stems, half the zest, and 4 cups hot water, then

boil.

2. Reduce heat to low and simmer covered for 15 minutes, stirring occasionally until rice is tender and chicken is cooked.

3. Turn off the heat.

4. Transfer chicken to a board and shred using 2 forks; one holding the chicken and the other pulling the meat.

5. In a heatproof bowl, whisk the eggs and lemon juice together.

6. Add 1 cup broth from the pot to the bowl and whisk again.

7. Repeat step 6 and whisk again.

8. Return broth to a gentle simmer over low heat.

9. Add shredded chicken and cook for 2 minutes to heat through, then remove pan from heat.

10. Gradually add egg mixture, stirring constantly until broth becomes glossy. Season.

11. Divide soup among bowls.

12. Ladle into soup bowls and scatter with dill leaves.

13. Drizzle with oil, then sprinkle with remaining zest and basil. Enjoy.

### *Smoked Cod and Potato Soup with Peas*

This creamy soup has tantalizing aromas that waft through the kitchen while poaching.

**Time:** 35 minutes

**Serving Size:** 1 | 2 | 4 servings

**Prep Time:** 10 minutes

**Cook Time:** 20 minutes

**Nutritional Facts/Info:**

Calories 301

Carbs 34.9 g

Fat 8.4 g

Protein 22.7 g

## Ingredients:

- 1 | 2 | 4 medium potatoes (sliced)
- ⅓ tsp | ¼ | ½ tbsp extra virgin olive oil
- ¼ | ½ | 1 onion (sliced)
- ⅛ | ¼ | ½ leek (washed, trimmed, sliced)
- ½ | 1 | 2 rashers bacon (rind and fat trimmed, chopped)
- ½ | 1 | 2 large fillets smoked cod (the orange type)
- 1 | 2 | 4 cups unsweetened almond milk
- 1 tbsp | 2 tbsp | ¼ cup white wine (optional)
- 1 | 2 | 4 rosemary sprigs
- 2 tbsp | ¼ | ½ cup frozen peas
- ¼ | ½ | 1 tbsp thyme leaves (picked)

## Directions:

1. In a saucepan of salted boiling water, add the potato and bring to a boil, then simmer until just tender. Drain.
2. In a large frying pan over medium-high heat, add the oil and cook the onion, leek, and bacon for several minutes.
3. Add the potatoes and rosemary sprigs, then pour in milk and wine. Crack with pepper.
4. Move the veggies aside in the pan, then lay in the fish.
5. Simmer gently uncovered for 5 minutes, then slice the fish in half widthwise with an egg flip.
6. Gently turn over, add the peas, then continue to poach until the fish flakes with a fork.
7. Ladle into soup bowls, breaking up the fish into bite-sized portions, then dust with thyme. Enjoy.

SALADS

### *Greek Salad with Crispy Feta*

A bright and colorful dish that is appetizing on its own or served as a side with fish or meat.

**Time:** 20 minutes

**Serving Size:** 1 | 2 | 4 servings

**Prep Time:** 15 minutes

**Cook Time:** 5 minutes

**Nutritional Facts/Info:**

Calories 195

Carbs 15.7 g

Fat 9.8 g

Protein 15.1 g

**Ingredients:**

- 50 | 100 | 200 g low-fat feta (quartered)
- ½ | 1 | 2 tbsp extra virgin olive oil
- 60 | 125 | 250 g mini Roma tomatoes (halved)
- 50 | 100 | 200 g yellow grape tomatoes (halved)
- ¼ | ½ | 1 green capsicum (deseeded, chopped)
- ¼ | ½ | 1 medium cucumber (chopped)
- ½ | 1 | 2 celery sticks (sliced)
- ⅛ | ¼ | ½ red onion (sliced into thin rings)
- 2 tbsp | ¼ | ½ cup pitted kalamata olives
- 1 tbsp | 2 tbsp | ¼ cup fresh oregano leaves
- 1 tbsp | 2 tbsp | ¼ cup fresh sage leaves
- ½ | 1 | 2 tbsp lemon juice
- ¼ | ½ | 1 garlic clove (crushed)
- ¼ | ½ | 1 tbsp flat leaf parsley (chopped)

**Directions:**

1. Pat feta dry with a paper towel.
2. Heat 2 tsp oil in a nonstick frying pan over high heat.

3. Add feta pieces and cook for 2 minutes on one side until crisp and golden.
4. Remove pan from the stove, leaving the feta to stand without moving for 10 minutes.
5. While the feta is cooling, add the tomatoes, capsicum, cucumber, celery, onion, olives, and half the oregano and sage leaves to a large bowl, then mix together.
6. Pour the lemon juice, garlic, parsley, and remaining oil into a small bowl. Season and whisk to combine.
7. Add dressing to the salad bowl, then toss to coat. Transfer to a serving platter.
8. Arrange the feta golden side up on the salad.
9. Sprinkle with remaining herbs and serve.

### Tuna Penne Salad

Quick and easy to prepare, this salad is just as easy to eat for lunch or dinner.

**Time:** 40 minutes

**Serving Size:** 1 | 2 | 4 servings

**Prep Time:** 20 minutes

**Cook Time:** 20 minutes

**Nutritional Facts/Info:**

Calories 326

Carbs 31.5 g

Fat 9.7 g

Protein 29.7 g

**Ingredients:**

- 85 | 175 | 375 g buckwheat penne
- 105 | 210 | 425 g can tuna in extra virgin olive oil (drained)

- ¼ | ½ | ¾ cup flat-leaf parsley (chopped)
- ¼ | ½ | 1 small red onion (halved, finely sliced)
- 30 | 60 | 120 g pitted kalamata olives (halved)
- ¼ | ½ | 1 red capsicum (seeded, sliced thinly)
- 65 | 135 | 275 g marinated artichoke hearts (drained)
- ¼ | ½ | 1 red chili (deseeded, finely sliced)
- 15 | 30 | 60 g rocket leaves
- 10 | 20 | 40 g pine nuts (toasted)

Lemon dressing:

- 25 | 50 | 100 g fat-free mayonnaise
- 10 | 20 | 40 ml lemon juice
- ½ | 1| 2 tsp Dijon mustard

## Directions:

1. In a saucepan of boiling salted water, cook the pasta until firm to bite. Drain.
2. Whisk the lemon dressing ingredients together in a jug and set aside.
3. Stir the pasta and lemon dressing together in a large bowl.
4. Add the tuna, parsley, olives, capsicum, chili, and artichokes, then gently toss to combine.
5. Arrange the salad onto a serving plate or individual plates.
6. Scatter the rocket and pine nuts over the top of the salad. Enjoy.

## *Quinoa Salad with Halloumi and Nectarines*

The quintessential low-calorie salad for warmer weather is here for you to try. You won't be disappointed!

**Time:** 30 minutes

**Serving Size:** 1 | 2 | 4 servings

**Prep Time:** 15 minutes

**Cook Time:** 10 minutes

**Nutritional Facts/Info:**

Calories 269

Carbs 23.9 g

Fat 15.7 g

Protein 10.6 g

**Ingredients:**

- 1 tbsp | 2 tbsp | ¼ cup tri-color quinoa
- 1 tbsp | 2 tbsp | ¼ cup extra virgin olive oil
- 30 | 60 | 120 g halloumi (halved lengthwise, cut crosswise)
- 2 tbsp | ¼ | ½ tbsp capers (rinsed, drained, and roughly chopped)
- 1 tbsp | 2 tbsp | ¼ cup currants
- ¼ | ¼| ½ lemon (juiced, zested)
- A pinch | pinch | ¼ tsp nutmeg
- ½ tsp | ¼ | ½ tbsp pure honey
- 1 | 2 | 3 yellow nectarines (halved, destoned, and wedged)
- 15 | 30| 60 g baby spinach leaves
- ¼ | ½ | 1 tbsp slivered almonds (toasted)

**Directions:**

1. In a microwave-safe bowl, mix quinoa and 1 cup of water. Cover and cook on high for 5 minutes.
2. Stir, cover, and cook for a further 2 minutes.
3. Stand covered for 5 minutes, then fluff with a fork.
4. Meanwhile, in a medium frying pan over medium-high heat, add 1 tbsp oil.
5. Add halloumi and cook for 1 minute on each side until golden brown and crispy. Remove from pan and set aside on a paper towel-lined plate.
6. Add the capers to the frying pan and cook for 30 seconds or

until crispy.

7. Add currants, lemon juice, lemon zest, nutmeg, and honey, then cook, stirring for a further 30 seconds until combined.
8. Turn off heat, add remaining oil and stir through.
9. Toss together quinoa, nectarine, and spinach, then lay out on a serving plate or individual plates.
10. Place the halloumi alongside the salad.
11. Drizzle the dressing over the top, then scatter with the almonds. Enjoy.

### *Apple and Nut Salad*

An attractive, crunchy salad with a slightly sweet finish.

**Time:** 20 minutes

**Serving Size:** 1 | 2 | 4 servings

**Prep Time:** 10 minutes

**Cook Time:** 5 minutes

**Nutritional Facts/Info:**

Calories 266

Carbs 16.5 g

Fat 21.2 g

Protein 5.9 g

**Ingredients:**

- 1/12 | ⅙ | ⅓ medium red cabbage (finely shredded)
- 10 | 20 | 40 g baby spinach leaves
- 1/12 | ⅙ | ⅓ small red onion (sliced thin)
- ¼ | ½ | 1 cup flat-leaf parsley (picked)
- ¼ | ½ | 1 red apple (cored, sliced thin)
- 1 tbsp | 2 tbsp | ¼ cup extra virgin olive oil
- 1 tbsp | 2 tbsp | ¼ cup apple cider vinegar

- ⅓ | ⅔ | 1⅓ tbsp whole grain mustard
- ⅛ | ¼ | ½ tsp minced garlic
- ¼ | ½ | 1 tsp pure honey
- 1½ tbsp | 2½ tbsp | ⅓ cup pecans (toasted)
- 1 tbsp | 2 tbsp | ¼ cup pine nuts (toasted)
- ¼ | ½ | 1 tbsp almond flakes (to serve)
- ¼ | ½ | 1 tsp lemon thyme (picked, to serve)

## Directions:

1. Place cabbage, spinach, onion, parsley, and apple into a serving bowl and toss gently.
2. In a screw-top jar, add the oil, vinegar, mustard, garlic, and honey, then shake well to combine. Season to taste.
3. Add the pecans and pine nuts to a small nonstick frying pan, then toast, shaking for several minutes until fragrant.
4. Add to salad, then drizzle some of the dressing over the top.
5. Sprinkle with almond flakes and thyme.
6. Serve salad with remaining dressing.

### *Zesty Salad with Moroccan Cod*

This fish has a spicy coating that pairs beautifully with the refreshing citrus salad.

**Time:** 40 minutes

**Serving Size:** 1 | 2 | 4 servings

**Prep Time:** 20 minutes

**Cook Time:** 10 minutes

**Nutritional Facts/Info:**

Calories 328

Carbs 29 g

Fat 14.5 g

Protein 26 g

**Ingredients:**

- 1 | 2 | 4 x 120 g cod fillets (skin removed)
- ¼ | ½ | 1 tbsp Moroccan seasoning (Ras El Hanout)
- 1½ tbsp | 3 tbsp | ⅓ cup extra virgin olive oil
- ¼ | ½ | 1 tbsp pure honey
- ¼ | ½ | 1 tsp Dijon Mustard
- ¼ | ½ | 1 red grapefruit (peeled, segmented over a bowl reserving juice)
- ½ | 1 | 2 limes (peeled, segmented over a bowl reserving juice)
- ½ | 1 | 2 oranges (peeled, sliced)
- ¼ | ½ | 1 fennel bulb (trimmed, quartered, finely shaved with veggie peeler, and fronds reserved)
- 2 tbsp | ¼ | ½ cup coriander leaves (picked)
- 1 tbsp | 2 tbsp | ¼ cup mint leaves (picked)
- 2 tbsp | ¼ | ½ cup pomegranate seeds
- 1 tbsp | 2 tbsp | ¼ cup pecans (chopped)
- 50 | 100 | 200 g feta (crumbled)

**Directions:**

1. In a shallow bowl, add the cod, seasoning, and ¼ | ½ | 1 tbsp oil, then gently fold to coat. Set aside.
2. In a screw-top jar, add the honey, mustard, reserved citrus juices, and remaining oil, then shake well. Season.
3. Make the salad in a large bowl by adding the citrus fruit, fennel and fronds, coriander, mint, pomegranate arils, and pecans. Gently toss.
4. Set on medium-high, heat a non-stick frying pan, then add the cod. Cook 3 minutes each side until just cooked through and caramelized.
5. Plate up with the salad.
6. Top with feta and drizzled dressing. Enjoy.

### *Barbequed Vegetable Salad with Cashew Dressing*

A colorful and inviting addition to the dinner table with a delectable, creamy dressing.

**Time:** 35 minutes (plus overnight soaking)

**Serving Size:** 1 | 2 | 4 servings

**Prep Time:** 15 minutes

**Cook Time:** 20 minutes

**Nutritional Facts/Info:**

Calories 310

Carbs 26.1 g

Fat 22.7 g

Protein 6.6 g

**Ingredients:**

- Extra virgin olive oil cooking spray
- ¼ | ½ | 1 red capsicum (deseeded, cut into thick strips)
- ¼ | ½ | 1 yellow capsicum (deseeded, cut into thick strips)
- ½ | 1 | 2 red onions (wedged)
- 50 | 100 | 200 g pumpkin (peeled, sliced thinly)
- ¾ | 1½ | 3 eggplants (thinly sliced lengthwise)
- ½ | 1 | 2 zucchinis (sliced lengthwise)
- 70 | 140 | 280 g artichoke hearts (drained)

Dressing:

- ¼ | ¼ | ½ small avocado
- 1 tbsp | 2 tbsp | ¼ cup extra virgin olive oil
- ½ | 1 | 2 tbsp lemon juice
- 8 | 15 | 30 g unsalted cashews (soaked in water overnight and drained)
- ¼ | ½ | 1 tsp minced garlic
- Flat-leaf parsley, rosemary, and basil leaves (to serve)

**Directions:**

1. Process dressing ingredients with a little water until smooth. Season.
2. Heat barbeque grill or chargrill pan on high and spray with cooking spray.
3. Cook the vegetables in batches if required until tender and caramelized.
4. Transfer vegetables onto a serving plate, then sprinkle with the dressing.
5. Garnish with herbs and serve.

### *Watermelon Salad with Blue Cheese*

A refreshing salad perfect for hot summer days with a hit of blue cheese and nutty crunch. Pairs well with barbequed fish or chicken.

**Time:** 15 minutes

**Serving Size:** 1 | 2 | 4 servings

**Prep Time:** 15 minutes

**Nutritional Facts/Info:**

Calories 236

Carbs 6.2 g

Fat 21.1 g

Protein 5.6 g

**Ingredients:**

- 160 | 325 | 650 g seedless watermelon (skinned, diced)
- ¼ | ½ | 1 Lebanese cucumber (ends trimmed, diced)
- 1 tbsp | ⅛ | ¼ red onion (diced)
- ¼ | ½ | 1 avocado (diced)
- 15 | 30 | 60 g pitted kalamata olives
- 2 tbsp | ¼ | ½ cup mint leaves (torn)

- 25 | 50 | 100 g mild blue cheese (crumbled)
- ½ | 1 | 2 tsp extra virgin olive oil
- ½ | 1 | 2 tsp red wine vinegar
- ¼ | ½ | 1 tbsp flat leaf parsley (chopped)
- 15 | 30 | 60 g walnuts (chopped)

## Directions:

1. Add watermelon, cucumber, onion, and olives to a large bowl and season. (If making in advance, leave adding the watermelon until just before serving.)
2. Add the mint, avocado, and blue cheese, then toss gently.
3. Combine the olive oil, vinegar, and parsley in a cup, then pour over the salad.
4. Divide among serving plates and sprinkle with the walnuts. Enjoy.

**Lamb and Lentil Salad with Fried Halloumi**

An attractive salad set off by the delicious lamb and fried halloumi.

**Time:** 25 minutes

**Serving Size:** 1 | 2 | 4 servings

**Prep Time:** 10 minutes

**Cook Time:** 10 minutes

**Nutritional Facts/Info:**

Calories 319

Carbs 10.2 g

Fat 18 g

Protein 28.1 g

**Ingredients:**

- Extra virgin olive oil spray
- 100 | 200 | 400 g lamb leg steaks (trimmed)
- 50 | 100 | 200 g halloumi (thickly sliced)
- 1 | 2 | 4 cups mixed salad leaves
- ½ | 1 | 2 cups mixed grape tomatoes (halved)
- 100 | 200 | 400 g canned lentils (rinsed, drained)
- 2 tbsp | ¼ | ½ cup rosemary leaves (picked, chopped)
- 1 tbsp | 2 tbsp | ¼ cup balsamic dressing
- ½ | 1 | 2 tbsp flaked almonds

**Directions:**

1. Heat a chargrill pan on medium-high heat.
2. Spray the lamb with oil. Season.
3. Cook for 3 mins each side or to your liking.
4. Sit on a plate and cover with foil to rest.
5. Heat a frying pan over medium-high heat and spray with oil.
6. Cook halloumi for 1 min each side until golden, then remove to a separate plate.
7. Thinly slice the lamb into bite-size pieces.
8. On a serving platter or individual plates, scatter the salad leaves, tomato, lentils, and rosemary.
9. Top with lamb and halloumi, then sprinkle with almonds.
10. Drizzle with dressing. Enjoy.

### Insalata Nizzarda (Pasta à la Niçoise)

A classic recipe originating from France, this dish is popular in the Mediterranean. Perfect to eat on a hot day or to take on a picnic.

**Time:** 30 minutes

**Serving Size:** 1 | 2 | 4 servings

**Prep Time:** 5 minutes

**Cook Time:** 15 minutes

**Nutritional Facts/Info:**

Calories 347

Carbs 55.1 g

Fat 18.7 g

Protein 19 g

**Ingredients:**

- 75 | 150 | 300 g whole wheat pasta shells or fusilli
- 35 | 75 | 150 g green beans (trimmed)
- 1 | 2 | 4 free-range eggs
- ½ | 1 | 2 tbsp extra virgin olive oil
- 50 | 100 | 200 g cherry tomatoes (halved)
- 2 tbsp | ¼ | ½ cup sliced kalamata olives
- 1½ | 3 | 6 anchovy fillets in oil (chopped)
- 12 | 25 | 50 g snow peas (trimmed, sliced in half lengthwise)
- ⅛ | ¼ | ½ lemon (juiced)
- ¼ | ½ | 1 tbsp pure honey
- ½ | 1 | 2 tsp Dijon mustard
- ¼ | ½ | 1 tbsp flat-leaf parsley leaves (to serve)
- ¼ | ½ | 1 tbsp fresh basil leaves (to serve)

**Directions:**

1. In a large saucepan of salted boiling water, cook the pasta until firm to bite.
2. Add the beans for the last 3 minutes of cooking. Drain.
3. Rinse the pasta and beans under cold water. Drain.

4. Meanwhile, bring a small saucepan of water to a boil, then add the eggs to cook for 6 minutes.
5. Drain and rinse under cold water.
6. When cool enough to handle, peel and slice thickly.
7. In a large bowl, add the cooked ingredients with the tomatoes, olives, anchovies, and snow peas, then gently mix together.
8. To make the vinaigrette, whisk the olive oil, lemon juice, honey, and mustard in a jug. Season and drizzle over the salad.
9. On a serving platter or individual plates, add the salad, then top with the sliced eggs.
10. Sprinkle with basil, parsley leaves, and cracked pepper. Enjoy.

### *Roast Pumpkin Chickpea Salad*

A lovely side addition to a meal or great cold as a snack that keeps well chilled in airtight containers.

**Time:** 40 minutes

**Serving Size:** 1 | 2 | 4 servings

**Prep Time:** 15 minutes

**Cook Time:** 25 minutes

**Nutritional Facts/Info:**

Calories 124

Carbs 21.7 g

Fat 3.1 g

Protein 4 g

**Ingredients:**

- 100 | 200 | 400 g pumpkin (peeled, cut into ½ in/1½ cm dice)
- Extra virgin olive oil spray
- ½ | 1 | 2 tsp lemon juice
- ¼ | ½ | 1 tsp pure honey

- ½ | 1 | 2 tsp extra virgin olive oil
- 106 | 212 | 425 g canned chickpeas (rinsed, drained)
- ¼ | ½ | 1 tbsp flat-leaf parsley (chopped)

**Directions:**

1. Set oven to 400 °F/200 °C or 350 °F/180 °C, fan forced. Line a baking tray with parchment paper.
2. Scatter pumpkin on tray, then spray lightly with oil.
3. Bake for 25 minutes until the pumpkin is tender and caramelized. Remove and set aside.
4. In a large bowl, whisk juice, oil, and honey together.
5. Add chickpeas, parsley, and pumpkin. Gently toss, then serve.

### *Smoked Salmon, Fennel, and Avocado Salad*

This tantalizing salad presents beautifully on a large platter for lunch with friends. Just double the recipe for more people. There are rarely any leftovers!

**Time:** 40 minutes

**Serving Size:** 1 | 2 | 4 servings

**Prep Time:** 25 minutes

**Cook Time:** 15 minutes

**Nutritional Facts/Info:**

Calories 371

Carbs 19.1 g

Fat 24.9 g

Protein 5.4 g

**Ingredients:**

- 65 | 125 | 250 g smoked salmon fillets (skinned, flaked into large chunks)
- 1 | 2 | 4 small potatoes (washed, sliced into ⅛ in/3 cm rounds)
- ¼ | ½ | 1 avocado (sliced, sprinkled with lemon juice)
- 40 | 75 | 150 g light sour cream
- ¼ | ½ | 1 tsp horseradish or horseradish cream
- 1 | 2 | 4 cups mixed salad leaves
- ¼ | ½ | 1 fennel bulb (trimmed, halved, and sliced finely)
- Extra virgin olive oil (to drizzle)
- 10 | 20 | 40 g mixed seeds and nuts (to serve)
- Fennel fronds (to serve)

Vinaigrette:

- 15 | 30 | 60 ml lemon juice
- ½ | 1 | 2 tsp extra virgin olive oil
- ¼ | ½ | 1 tsp whole grain mustard
- ¼ | ½ | 1 tsp minced garlic
- 1 pinch sugar
- 1 pinch salt and pepper

## Directions:

1. Place the potato slices in salted boiling water and cook gently until tender. Remove from pot and place on paper towel in one layer to cool.
2. Mix the ingredients for the vinaigrette, then set aside.
3. In a small bowl, mix the sour cream and horseradish together. Taste and add a little more if there's no horseradish bite to the cream.
4. Line the middle of a large serving plate with the potatoes.
5. Drizzle lightly with olive oil and season.
6. Using a teaspoon, dot the potatoes with half the cream.
7. Add the avocado on top of the potatoes and dot with the rest of the cream.

8. In a large bowl, add the mixed salad leaves and fennel slices together.
9. Add enough vinaigrette to lightly coat the salad and gently toss.
10. Lightly scatter the salad leaves over the top of the potato and avocado, building height as you go.
11. Arrange the smoked salmon pieces across the top of the salad.
12. Sprinkle with the mixed seeds and nuts.
13. Arrange the fennel fronds across the top and serve.

### *Quinoa Salad with Summer Fruit*

A terrific change for a healthy low-calorie lunch with colorful flavor pops throughout.

**Time:** 45 minutes

**Serving Size:** 1 | 2 | 4 servings

**Prep Time:** 10 minutes

**Cook Time:** 25 minutes

**Nutritional Facts/Info:**

Calories 230

Carbs 25.7 g

Fat 9.9 g

Protein 9.9 g

**Ingredients:**

- ¼ | ½ | 1 cup tri-color quinoa
- ⅛ | ¼ | ½ small red onion (sliced thinly)
- 15 | 30 | 60 g baby rocket leaves (arugula)
- 2 | 4 | 8 strawberries (sliced)
- 30 | 60 | 125 g seedless green grapes
- 30 | 60 | 125 g blueberries

- 30 | 60 | 100 g low-fat feta (drained, crumbled)
- 1 tbsp | 2 tbsp | ⅓ cup toasted sliced almonds
- 1 tbsp | 2 tbsp | ¼ cup low-fat balsamic dressing

## Directions:

1. Bring the quinoa and ⅜ | ¾ | 1½ cups boiling water to boil over high heat. Turn heat to low and cover.
2. Simmer for 15 minutes or until liquid is absorbed and the kernels have popped. Remove from heat.
3. Set aside covered for 10 minutes to steam.
4. Fluff with a fork, then tip into a large bowl. Set aside to cool.
5. Add red onion, rocket, strawberries, grapes, blueberries, feta, and almonds to the quinoa. Season and toss to combine.
6. Divide the quinoa salad among serving plates or lunch boxes.
7. Drizzle the balsamic dressing over the salad, or if making for lunch, divide into 4 small containers.
8. Serve or refrigerate until required.

MAIN MEALS

### *Layered Polenta with Roasted Mediterranean Vegetables*

This tasty dish is loaded with fresh flavor that your family will enjoy.

**Time:** 1 hour 5 minutes

**Serving Size:** 1 | 2 | 4 servings

**Prep Time:** 25 minutes

**Cook Time:** 40 minutes

**Nutritional Facts/Info:**

Calories 267

Carbs 18.2 g

Fat 17.3 g

Protein 10.9 g

## Ingredients:

- 125 | 250 | 500 ml chicken stock
- ¼ | ½ | 1 cup polenta
- ¼ | ½ | 1 tbsp extra virgin olive oil, plus extra to drizzle
- 2 tbsp | ¼ cup | ½ cup low-fat parmesan cheese (finely grated)
- 25 | 50 | 100 g goat's cheese (crumbled)
- 35 | 70 | 140 g green or yellow capsicums (deseeded, quartered)
- ½ | 1 | 2 zucchinis (thickly sliced into rounds)
- Extra virgin olive oil spray
- 25 | 50 | 100 g cherry or grape tomatoes (halved)
- ½ | 1 | 2 garlic cloves (sliced thinly)
- 2 | 3 | 6 fresh oregano leaves
- 2 | 3 | 6 sprigs fresh thyme
- Balsamic glaze (to serve)

## Directions:

1. Grease a loaf tin, then line the base and sides with parchment paper. Extend the paper above the pan on all sides to make removal easy.
2. Pour stock and the same amount of water into a large saucepan over high heat. Bring to a boil.
3. Add polenta, stirring constantly in a slow, steady stream. Reduce heat to low.
4. Cook, stirring for 6–7 minutes or until thick. Remove from heat.
5. Stir in olive oil and parmesan cheese. Season.
6. Spread half the polenta into the prepared loaf tin.
7. Sprinkle with half the goat's cheese.
8. Spread remaining polenta over cheese, then sprinkle with remaining cheese.
9. Refrigerate for 4 hours or until firm.
10. When ready to cook, remove the polenta from the fridge.
11. Set oven to 200 °C/400 °F or 180 °C/360 °F, fan forced. Line 1

baking tray with parchment paper and spray another tray with olive oil.

12. Place the zucchini and capsicum on the lined tray and drizzle with olive oil. Season and toss to coat.

13. Roast for 20 minutes.

14. Add tomatoes, garlic, oregano, and thyme sprigs to the vegetables. Spray with olive oil, then cook for 10 minutes or until tender.

15. In the meantime, carefully remove the polenta from the loaf tin, then place on the remaining baking tray. Spray with olive oil.

16. Bake for 12–15 minutes or until crisp and golden. Transfer to a serving board.

17. Top with roasted vegetables, thyme, and oregano.

18. Drizzle with balsamic glaze. Slice and serve.

### *Lemon and Ricotta Pasta with Zucchini*

A delightfully light and delicate pasta dish with tangy flavor. Any type of pasta can be used in this dish.

**Time:** 25 minutes

**Serving Size:** 1 | 2 | 4 servings

**Prep Time:** 10 minutes

**Cook Time:** 15 minutes

**Nutritional Facts/Info:**

Calories 326

Carbs 24.9 g

Fat 22.2 g

Protein 9.3 g

**Ingredients:**

- 75 | 150 | 300 g wholemeal pasta
- 1¼ tbsp | 2½ tbsp | ⅓ cup extra virgin olive oil
- ½ | 1 | 2 zucchinis (ends removed, sliced into ⅛ in/3 cm rounds)
- 1 | 2 | 3 garlic cloves (thinly sliced)
- 15 | 25 | 50 g baby spinach
- ¼ | ½ | 1 tbsp lemon zest (finely sliced)
- ¼ | ½ | 1 small chili (seeds removed, sliced finely)
- 1 | 2 | 4 tbsp flat-leaf parsley (chopped finely)
- 32 | 65 | 130 g low-fat ricotta
- 1 | 2 | 4 pinches shaved parmesan cheese

## Directions:

1. Cook the pasta in boiling salted water until al dente. Drain, reserving 1 cup of water from the pot.
2. Return the pasta to the pot off the heat.
3. While the pasta is cooking, heat a frying pan on medium heat, add the oil and cook the zucchini in batches until golden on each side. Remove to a paper towel.
4. Add the garlic and sauté for 30 seconds, stirring, then add the zucchini back into the pan.
5. Add the spinach, lemon zest, chili, parsley, and 2 tbsp | ¼ | ½ cup of the pasta water to the pan.
6. Season and simmer until the spinach wilts.
7. Add the cooked pasta to the pan and toss with the other ingredients. If the mixture seems dry, add a little more pasta water and toss.
8. Gently stir through the ricotta, then take off the heat.
9. Serve garnished with flat-leaf parsley and parmesan.

### *Fish Patties with Bean and Tomato Salad*

This lip-smacker is a tastier, healthier alternative to fish and chips.

**Time:** 1 hour

**Serving Size:** 1 | 2 | 4 servings

**Prep Time:** 35 minutes

**Cook Time:** 25 minutes

**Nutritional Facts/Info:**

Calories 460

Carbs 57.9 g

Fat 16.1 g

Protein 22.6 g

**Ingredients:**

- 175 | 350 | 700 g potatoes (peeled, chopped)
- 55 | 110 | 2 x 110 g cans skinless/boneless mackerel fillets in olive oil or similar (drained)
- ¾ | 1½ | 3 scallions (chopped)
- 2 tbsp | ¼ | ½ cup basil leaves (chopped)
- ¼ | ½ | 1 tbsp parsley (chopped)
- ½ | 1 | 2 tbsp sliced kalamata olives
- ¼ | ½ | 1 tsp lemon rind (finely grated)
- 1 small | 1 medium | 1 lg free-range egg (lightly whisked)
- 15 | 35 | 70 g whole-wheat panko breadcrumbs
- ½ | 1 | 2 tbsp parmesan cheese (finely grated)
- Extra virgin olive oil (for shallow frying)

Tomato and Cannellini Bean Salad:

- 50| 100 | 200 g grape tomatoes (halved)
- 100 | 200 | 400 g cannellini beans (rinsed, drained)
- ¼ | ½ | 2 tsp fresh oregano leaves (chopped)
- ¼ | ½ | 1 gem or cos lettuce (leaves separated)
- ¼ | ½ | 2 tbsp balsamic vinegar dressing
- Lemon wedges (to serve)

**Directions:**

1. Place potatoes in a large saucepan of cold water and bring to a boil.
2. Cook for 12 minutes or until tender. Drain.
3. Return the pan of potatoes to low heat and toss until the liquid evaporates. Take off heat.
4. Roughly mash in the pot. Transfer to a bowl and set aside.
5. Add the mackerel, scallions, basil, parsley, kalamata olives, lemon rind, egg, and half the breadcrumbs to the potato. Season, then stir to combine.
6. Using damp hands, shape mixture into 2 | 4 | 8 patties.
7. Place the remaining breadcrumbs in a shallow dish with the parmesan. Mix together.
8. Coat the patties in breadcrumbs, then place on a parchment paper-lined plate.
9. Chill until ready to cook.
10. To make the tomato bean salad, add the tomato, beans, oregano, and lettuce in a bowl, then mix together.
11. Drizzle over the balsamic dressing and gently toss.
12. Pour enough oil into a large nonstick frying pan to measure just under ½ in/1 cm. Heat over medium heat.
13. Shallow fry patties for 2–3 minutes each side or until golden and crisp. Drain on paper towel.
14. Serve the patties with the salad and lemon wedges.

### *Vegetarian Paella with Tofu*

We've used bulgur as an alternative in this tasty paella with pea pops and silky tofu to balance the textures.

**Time:** 40 minutes

**Serving Size:** 1 | 2 | 4 servings

**Prep Time:** 15 minutes

**Cook Time:** 30 minutes

**Nutritional Facts/Info:**

Calories 298

Carbs 49.3 g

Fat 7.5 g

Protein 15 g

**Ingredients:**

- ¼ | ½ | 1 tbsp extra virgin olive oil
- ¼ | ½ | 1 onion (diced)
- ½ | 1 | 2 cloves garlic (diced)
- ¼ | ½ | 1 cup bulgur wheat
- ¼ | ½ | 1 tbsp smoked paprika
- ¾ | 1½ | 3 cups vegetable stock
- 1½ | 3 | 6 Roma tomatoes (diced)
- 75 | 150 | 300 g firm tofu (halved horizontally lengthwise like a sandwich, into thirds lengthwise, then cut into fifths crosswise for 30 pieces)
- ⅜ | ¾ | 1½ cup frozen baby peas
- ½ | 1 | 2 bell peppers (deseeded, diced)
- 2 tbsp | ¼ | ½ cup parsley (to serve)
- ¼ | ½ | 1 spring onion (sliced, to serve)
- ¼ | ½ | 1 lemon (wedged, to serve)

**Directions:**

1. In a large saucepan over medium heat, add the oil.
2. Add garlic and onion, then sauté for 2 minutes.
3. Add bulgur and paprika, then cook 2 minutes, shaking the pan to coat the bulgar.
4. Add stock, stir through, then cover, cooking for 7 minutes.
5. Uncover, add tomatoes, and cook 20 minutes until bulgur is tender.
6. Meanwhile, add boiling water and 2 generous pinches of salt to a medium saucepan, then gently boil and turn down.
7. Carefully slide the tofu cubes into the water.

8. Simmer for 3 minutes, then turn heat off to leave tofu steeping.
9. Add peas and peppers to the paella, then cook 2 minutes until heated through.
10. Transfer the drained tofu to the paella, then stir gently and crack with pepper.
11. Sprinkle with parsley and spring onions, then serve with lemon wedges.

### *Speedy Seafood Spaghetti*

This classic recipe has a touch of chili and is so delectable, your family will be asking for seconds.

**Time:** 30 minutes

**Serving Size:** 1 | 2 | 4 servings

**Prep Time:** 10 minutes

**Cook Time:** 20 minutes

**Nutritional Facts/Info:**

Calories 539

Carbs 68 g

Fat 5.5 g

Protein 43.9 g

**Ingredients:**

- 85 | 175 | 350 g wholemeal spaghetti
- 15 | 25 | 45 g anchovy fillets (drained)
- 1 | 2 | 4 cloves garlic (crushed)
- 2 tbsp | ¼ | ½ tsp dried chili flakes
- 2 tbsp | ¼ | ½ cup white wine (optional, or vegetable stock)
- 200 | 405 | 810 g crushed tomatoes

- 100 | 200 | 400 g seafood marinara mix (shrimp, calamari, mussels, and oysters)
- 1½ tbsp | 3 tbsp | ⅓ cup fresh parsley (chopped)
- 1½ tbsp | 3 tbsp | ⅓ cup fresh basil (chopped)
- 35 | 75 | 150 g mixed salad leaves (or Italian style salad kit)
- 3 | 6 | 12 cherry tomatoes
- ¼ | ½ | 1 tbsp extra virgin olive oil
- ¼ | ½ | 1 lemon (juiced, zested)
- Shaved parmesan (to serve)

## Directions:

1. In a pot of salted boiling water, cook the pasta until firm to bite. Drain.
2. Meanwhile, in a large deep frying pan over medium-high heat, add anchovies, including oil, then sauté for 1 minute.
3. Add garlic and chili, then sauté for 1 minute.
4. Add wine or stock, then bring to a boil.
5. Add tomatoes and stir, bringing to a boil again.
6. Turn heat down to medium, then simmer uncovered for 5 minutes.
7. Add seafood and continue to cook for 4 minutes until just cooked.
8. Add pasta and toss to coat.
9. In the meantime, prepare the salad by mixing the salad leaves, cherry tomatoes, and parmesan together.
10. Mix the oil, lemon juice, and zest in a cup, then pour over the salad. Toss.
11. Portion the pasta onto plates, then scatter with herbs.
12. Serve with the salad.

### Chickpea and Quinoa Burgers with Herb Yogurt

These low-fat patties are a quick, easy, and satisfying meal the whole family will appreciate.

**Time:** 35 minutes

**Serving Size:** 1 | 2 | 4 servings

**Prep Time:** 15 minutes

**Cook Time:** 20 minutes

**Nutritional Facts/Info:**

Calories 421

Carbs 46.6 g

Fat 21 g

Protein 14.5 g

**Ingredients:**

- 1 | 2 | 4 scallions (sliced)
- ½ |1 | 2 garlic cloves (chopped finely)
- ½ | 1 | 1½ cups cooked quinoa
- 100 | 200 | 400 g can chickpeas (rinsed, drained)
- 1 | 1 | 2 free-range eggs
- 2 tbsp | ¼ | ½ cup parsley (chopped)
- 2 tbsp | ¼ | ½ cup wholemeal breadcrumbs

Herb Yogurt:

- ⅛ | ¼ | ½ avocado
- 1 | 2 | 4 tbsp extra virgin olive oil
- ¼ | ½ | 1½ tbsp apple cider vinegar
- ¼ | ½ | 1½ tbsp lemon juice
- 1 | 2 | 4 tbsp mixed herbs like chives, basil, and parsley
- 1 ½ | 3 | 6 tbsp low-fat Greek yogurt

Tomato Salad:

- 1 | 2 | 4 vine-ripened tomatoes (chopped)
- 50 | 100 | 200 g colored cherry tomatoes (halved)
- ¼ | ½ | 1 cucumber (diced)

- ¼ | ¼ | ½ small red onion (finely sliced)
- Baby rocket leaves (to serve)

## Directions:

1. In a processor, combine half the scallions and garlic, quinoa, chickpeas, parsley, and eggs. Spoon into a bowl.
2. Stir in the breadcrumbs and season.
3. With wet hands, shape ⅓ cup portions into 2 | 4 | 8 burgers.
4. On medium-high heat, pour half the oil in a frying pan, then fry the burgers, turning once for 6–8 minutes until caramelized.
5. Meantime, process the vinegar, avocado, lemon juice, herbs, yogurt, and remaining scallions, garlic, and oil until smooth. Season.
6. Combine tomatoes, onion, and cucumber in a bowl.
7. Serve burgers dressed with salad, dressing, and topped with rocket leaves.

### *Tomato and Saffron Pasta with Pangrattato*

A full-flavored pasta finished beautifully with the addition of crispy pangrattato.

**Time:** 35 minutes

**Serving Size:** 1 | 2 | 4 servings

**Prep Time:** 15 minutes

**Cook Time:** 20 minutes

**Nutritional Facts/Info:**

Calories 221

Carbs 18.5 g

Fat 14.8 g

Protein 4.4 g

**Ingredients:**

- 125 | 250 | 500 g roma tomatoes (skinned, diced finely)
- ½ | 1 | 2 cloves garlic (finely diced)
- ¼ | ½ | 1 large pinch of saffron threads
- 45 | 90 | 180 ml extra virgin olive oil
- 1 | 2 | 3 tbsp flat leaf parsley (torn)
- 3 | 6 | 12 basil leaves (torn)
- 2 | 4 | 6 tarragon leaves (torn)
- 65 | 125 | 250 g wholemeal pasta
- 1 | 2 | 4 pinches grated parmesan (to serve)

Pangrattato:

- 15 | 30 | 60 ml extra virgin olive oil
- 20 | 35 | 70 g wholemeal breadcrumbs (fine)
- ½ | 1 | 2 tbsp flat leaf parsley (chopped)

**Directions:**

1. In a bowl, add the tomato, saffron, garlic, basil, parsley, and tarragon. Cover and refrigerate for at least one hour, then take out before starting to cook. (This can be done ahead of time.)

2. To make the pangrattato, heat a small pan to medium heat and add the oil.
3. Add the breadcrumbs and keep stirring until golden.
4. Add the parsley and stir. Take off the stove.
5. In a large pot of boiling salted water, cook the pasta until firm to bite. Drain and pour into a serving bowl.
6. Add the tomato saffron sauce to the bowl and gently stir through the pasta.
7. Sprinkle the pangrattato and parmesan over the top. Enjoy.

### Roast Vegetables with Garlic Mustard Anchovy Oil

Served as a main or side dish, not only is this an appetizing way to eat vegetables—especially in winter—but a practical way to use older veggies. A time-saving bonus is no peeling, as they are cooked in their skin.

**Time:** 1 hour 10 minutes

**Serving Size:** 1 | 2 | 4 servings

**Prep Time:** 10 minutes

**Cook Time:** 1 hour

**Nutritional Facts/Info:**

Calories 396

Carbs 64.1 g

Fat 13.3 g

Protein 12.1 g

**Ingredients:**

- 1 | 2 | 4 medium carrots
- 1 | 2 | 4 medium parsnips
- 1 | 2 | 4 medium onions (halved)
- 1 | 2 | 4 medium beetroot

- ¼ | ½ | 1 medium cauliflower (quartered)
- ½ | 1 | 2 large heads of garlic
- ½ | 1 | 2 leeks
- 2 | 4 | 6 sprigs fresh rosemary
- ¼ | ½ | 1 cup extra virgin olive oil
- 1 | 2 | 4 anchovies (finely chopped)
- 1 | 2 | 4 garlic cloves (chopped finely)
- ½ | 1 | 2 tsp Dijon mustard
- ½ | 1 | 2 tsp capers (rinsed, chopped)
- 1 | 2 | 4 tbsp chives (finely chopped)
- ¼ | ½ | 1 tbsp parsley (chopped finely)
- 1 | 2 | 4 slices crusty wholemeal bread

## Directions:

1. Set oven to 400 °F/200 °C. Line an oven tray with parchment paper.
2. In a bowl, combine the oil, garlic, anchovies, mustard, and capers. Set aside.
3. Spread the vegetables on the tray, leaving room between each one.
4. Brush the vegetables with oil, season, and sprinkle with rosemary. Place in the oven.
5. Cook for 30 minutes, then shake the oven tray to move the vegetables around.
6. Cook for another 30 minutes, then check the vegetables are tender with a fork. When they are wrinkled and caramelized, they are ready.
7. Take the vegetables out of the oven and sprinkle with the herbs.
8. Serve in the baking tray with warm, crusty bread, making sure to squeeze the roasted garlic onto the bread.

### *Stuffed Mussels with Saffron Cream*

A timely dish to make—but worth the effort—that can also be served as hors d'oeuvres. One mussel is never enough, and frozen mussels in the shell may be used.

**Time:** 1 hour

**Serving Size:** 1 | 2 | 4 servings

**Prep Time:** 25 minutes

**Cook Time:** 25 minutes

**Nutritional Facts/Info:**

Calories 235

Carbs 19 g

Fat 13.1 g

Protein 11.1 g

**Ingredients:**

- ¼ | ½ | 1 kg green lip mussels (scraped, debearded)
- 1 tbsp | 2 tbsp | ¼ cup white wine
- ¼ | ½ | 1 tbsp extra virgin olive oil (plus extra for drizzling)
- ⅛ | ¼ | ½ red onion (diced)
- ¼ | ½ | 1 clove garlic (chopped fine)
- ½ | 1 | 2 tomatoes (deseeded, diced)
- ¼ | ½ | 1 red pepper (deseeded, diced)
- 5 | 10 | 20 g panko crumbs
- ¾ | 1½ | 3 tbsp flat-leaf parsley (chopped fine)
- ½ | 1 | 2 tsp parmesan (grated)

Saffron Cream:

- 2 tbsp | ¾ | 1½ tbsp extra virgin olive oil
- 2 tbsp | ¾ | 1½ tbsp wholemeal plain flour
- ½ | 1 | 2 cups unsweetened almond milk
- ⅛ | ¼ | ½ tsp lemon zest

- ¼ | ½ | 1 pinch saffron threads (soaked in 2 tsp hot water)

## Directions:

1. In a large saucepan over high heat, tip in the mussels and wine.
2. Cover and steam for a few minutes while shaking the pan until the mussels open.
3. Remove from heat and drain, reserving ¼ cup of liquid.
4. Remove flesh from the shells into a bowl, then discard half the shells.
5. Chop the mussel meat, cover, and chill.
6. Clean the shells, removing any meat with a teaspoon, then wash and dry on paper towels.
7. Set out the shells on a grilling tray.
8. In a frying pan, heat the oil, then sauté the onions and garlic until soft.
9. Add chopped tomatoes and peppers, then sauté until soft.
10. Add mussel liquid and simmer until almost evaporated. Season to taste, then add the mussel meat and cook for 2 minutes. Set aside.
11. In a small bowl, mix breadcrumbs, parsley, and parmesan. Set aside.
12. To make the saffron cream, add oil to a saucepan over low heat. Add flour and continuously stir for a few minutes with a wooden spoon.
13. Add the milk gradually while stirring until the sauce smooths and thickens.
14. Add the lemon zest and saffron with water. Season.
15. Set the oven grill on.
16. Stuff the mussels by adding 1 tbsp of mussel mixture to each shell.
17. Top with 2 tsp of saffron cream and sprinkled breadcrumbs.
18. Drizzle with a little oil.
19. Grill for 8–10 minutes until crumbs are golden. Enjoy.

### *Veggie Moussaka with Tzatziki*

A deliciously satisfying dish—without the meat—that takes us back to Greece.

**Time:** 1 hour 20 minutes

**Serving Size:** 1 | 2 | 4 servings

**Prep Time:** 15 minutes

**Cook Time:** 50 minutes

**Nutritional Facts/Info:**

Calories 313

Carbs 39.8 g

Fat 10.5 g

Protein 17.4 g

**Ingredients:**

- 1 tbsp | 2 tbsp | ¼ cup extra virgin olive oil
- ½ | ½ | 1 onion (chopped)
- 1 | 2 | 4 garlic cloves (crushed)
- ¼ | ½ | 1 tsp dried oregano
- 105 | 210 | 420 g tomatoes (crushed)
- 25 | 50 | 100 g baby spinach leaves
- 105 | 210 | 420 g can lentils (rinsed, drained)
- 50 | 100 | 200 g tzatziki (at room temperature)
- 1 free-range egg
- 25 | 50 | 100 g Greek feta (crumbled)
- ½ | ½ | 1 large eggplant (cut lengthwise into ⅜ in/1 cm slices)
- 50 | 100 | 200 g sweet potato (cut lengthwise into ⅜ in/1 cm slices)
- 2¼ tbsp | ⅓ | ⅔ cup low-fat mozzarella (shredded)
- 2 tbsp | ¼ | ½ cup fresh basil leaves (picked, to serve)

**Directions:**

1. Set oven to 350 °F/180 °C and grease a 10 x 12 in/20 x 30 cm roasting pan or casserole dish.
2. In a medium saucepan over medium heat, add 1 tbsp oil.
3. Add onion, garlic, and oregano, then cook for 5 minutes until soft.
4. Add tomatoes and lentils, then simmer for 5 minutes until starting to thicken.
5. Stir in spinach leaves. Set aside.
6. Whisk tzatziki, egg, and feta in a bowl. Set aside.
7. Brush both sides of the sweet potato and eggplant slices with remaining oil, then crack with pepper.
8. Heat a chargrill pan over medium-high heat.
9. Cook vegetables in batches for 3 minutes each side until charred. Transfer to a paper towel-lined plate.
10. Arrange a layer of eggplant in casserole dish.
11. Cover with one-third of the tomato sauce.
12. Top with sweet potato.
13. Repeat layering sauce and eggplant finishing with sauce.
14. Spread tzatziki mixture over sauce and scatter with mozzarella.
15. Bake for 30 minutes until golden.
16. Scatter with basil, cut into squares, then serve.

### Pan-Fried Lemon Mackerel

This is a quick and easy, yet satisfying meal that pleases everyone's taste buds.

**Time:** 30 minutes

**Serving Size:** 1 | 2 | 4

**Prep Time:** 10 minutes

**Cook Time:** 10 minutes

**Nutritional Facts/Info:**

Calories 346

Carbs 11.9 g

Fat 24.5 g

Protein 23.9 g

**Ingredients:**

- ¼ | ½ | 1 tbsp extra virgin olive oil
- 1 | 2 | 4 x 120 g mackerel fillets or white fish like cod (skin on)
- ½ | 1 | 2 cups baby spinach leaves
- ¼ | ½ | 1 cup baby arugula (rocket)
- ¼ | ½ | 1 cup beet leaves
- ½ | 1 | 2 scallions (thinly sliced on the slant)
- ¼ | ½ | 1 celery (sliced thin)
- 2 tbsp| ¼ | ½ cup flat leaf parsley (picked)
- ½ | 1 | 2 lemons (juiced, zested)
- ½ | 1 | 2 tsp whole grain mustard
- 1 tbsp | 2 tbsp | ¼ cup extra virgin avocado oil
- ¼ | ½ | 1 tbsp chopped hazelnuts
- ¼ | ½ | 1 tbsp flat leaf parsley (chopped)
- ¼ | ½ | 1 tbsp fresh dill (picked)
- ¼ | ½ | 1 lemon (cut into cheeks, to serve)

**Directions:**

1. In a serving bowl, add the spinach, arugula and beet leaves, spring onions, parsley, and celery. Gently toss, then set aside.
2. Heat 1 tbsp oil in a frying pan over medium heat.
3. Add the fish skin side down and cook until the flesh starts to turn white partway up the side.
4. Gently loosen the fish skin from the pan every now and then and turn over with an egg flip.
5. Sprinkle the fish with lemon juice, reserving ¼ cup, then cook until the flesh flakes slightly with a fork.
6. Remove from heat and transfer to a paper towel-lined plate.
7. Meanwhile, whisk remaining oil, ¼ cup lemon juice, and mustard in a jug.

8. Drizzle over the salad 1 tbsp at a time and toss.
9. Transfer fish to serving plates.
10. Scatter salad and lemon cheeks on the side.
11. Pepper the salad with hazelnuts.
12. Dress the fish with herbs and zest. Enjoy.

### *Aubergine Lasagne with Plant-Based Mince*

This vegetarian version of lasagne still ticks the boxes for flavor and is a healthier alternative to meat.

**Time:** 1 hour 35 minutes

**Serving Size:** 1 | 2 | 4 servings

**Prep Time:** 10 minutes

**Cook Time:** 1 hour 5 minutes

**Nutritional Facts/Info:**

Calories 341

Carbs 35.6 g

Fat 9.7 g

Protein 29.8 g

**Ingredients:**

- ¼ | ½ | 1 large eggplant (sliced lengthwise)
- Extra virgin olive oil spray
- ¼ | ½ | 1 tbsp extra virgin olive oil
- 100 | 200 | 400 g plant based mince
- 100 | 200 | 400 g diced tomatoes
- 2 tbsp | ¼ | ½ cup basil leaves (chopped)
- A pinch sugar
- 1 tbsp | 2 tbsp | ¼ cup wholemeal plain flour
- ½ | 1 | 2 cups unsweetened almond milk
- 2 tbsp | ¼ | ½ cup parmesan (grated)

- 25 | 50 | 100 g wholemeal lasagne pasta sheets
- ½ | 1 | 2 cups baby spinach leaves
- ¼ | ½ | 1 cup low-fat mozzarella (shredded)
- 1 | 2 | 4 cups mixed salad leaves
- 2 tbsp | ¼ | ½ cup mixed fresh herbs (picked)
- Balsamic dressing (to drizzle)
- ¼ cup pine nuts

## Directions:

1. Set oven to 350 °F/180 °C and spray a lasagne tray with oil.
2. In a large saucepan over medium heat, add the mince and stir until browned.
3. Add the tomatoes, basil, and a pinch of sugar, then stir. Bring to a boil, then simmer for 10 minutes covered.
4. Meanwhile, in a frying pan on medium, spray eggplant with oil, then cook for 3 minutes. Flip, spray, then continue to cook until caramelized.
5. Remove to a paper towel-lined plate.
6. To make the bechamel, add oil to a saucepan over medium heat.
7. Add flour and stir for 2 minutes until a paste forms.
8. Add milk gradually, whisking, then bring to a gentle boil.
9. Turn heat down, then simmer, stirring for 5 minutes.
10. Stir in 1 tbsp | 2 tbsp | ¼ cup parmesan and season. Remove from heat.
11. Cover tray with lasagne pasta sheets, breaking to fit where necessary.
12. Layer half each of mince sauce, eggplant, spinach, and bechamel sauce.
13. Repeat steps 11 and 12.
14. Scatter remaining parmesan and mozzarella over the top.
15. Bake for 45 minutes until cheese is golden brown. Remove from oven.
16. Prepare salad by mixing the salad leaves and herbs in a bowl, then drizzling with balsamic dressing.

17. Sprinkle with pine nuts.
18. Cut lasagne into slices and serve with the salad.

### *Funghi and Ricotta Pappardelle*

A welcome choice to make for a quick weeknight dinner.

**Time:** 25 minutes

**Serving Size:** 1 | 2 | 4 servings

**Prep Time:** 10 minutes

**Cook Time:** 15 minutes

**Nutritional Facts/Info:**

Calories 343

Carbs 29.1 g

Fat 15.4 g

Protein 26.8 g

**Ingredients:**

- ¼ | ½ | 1 tbsp extra virgin olive oil
- ½ | 1 | 2 cloves of garlic (chopped finely)
- ½ | 1 | 2 cloves of garlic (finely sliced)
- 12 | 25 | 50 g wholemeal breadcrumbs
- 3 | 5 | 10 g thyme leaves (picked)
- ¼ | ½ | 1 onion (diced)
- 100 | 200 | 400 g mixed mushrooms like cup, brown, swiss, or field (sliced)
- 75 | 150 | 300 g wholemeal pappardelle or tagliatelle
- ¼ | ½ | 1 cup low-fat feta cheese (drained)
- ¼ | ½ | 1 cup smooth low-fat ricotta
- 30 | 60 | 120 g baby spinach leaves
- ¼ | ½ | 1 tbsp parsley (chopped)
- 5 | 10 | 20 g parmesan (grated, to serve)

## Directions:

1. Place a large frying pan on medium-high heat with oil.
2. Add the chopped garlic, breadcrumbs, and half the thyme. Cook, stirring until golden, then spoon into a bowl.
3. Place the pan back on medium heat, adding the sliced garlic, onion, remaining thyme, and mushrooms. Cook for 8–10 minutes until golden.
4. In a large pot of salted boiling water, cook the pasta until firm to bite. Drain, reserving ½ cup of the pasta water.
5. Meanwhile, stir the feta, ricotta, spinach leaves, and half the parsley into the mushrooms. Simmer until the spinach wilts.
6. Add half the parmesan and season with pepper.
7. Add the pasta, then gently toss in the sauce, adding splashes of the cooking water to loosen if required.
8. Divide between bowls, then scatter with garlic crumb, remaining parsley, and parmesan.
9. Delicious served with wilted greens or a crisp garden salad.

### *Chargrilled Lamb with Roasted Cauliflower and Barley*

A low-calorie meal studded with pomegranate arils, offering tasty variety.

**Time:** 1 hour

**Serving Size:** 1 | 2 | 4 servings

**Prep Time:** 20 minutes

**Cook Time:** 40 minutes

**Nutritional Facts/Info:**

Calories 359

Carbs 26.1 g

Fat 19.1 g

Protein 21.8 g

## Ingredients:

- ¼ | ½ | 1 eggplant (cut into 1 inch/2 cm chunks)
- 125 | 250 | 500 g cauliflower (cut into florets)
- ½ | ¾ | 1½ tsp garam masala
- ½ | ½ | 1 tsp sesame seeds
- 30 | 60 | 120 g pearl barley
- ½ | 1 | 2 x 200g lamb backstraps (eye of loin, trimmed)
- Extra virgin olive oil spray
- 2 | 4 | 8 asparagus (soft ends snapped off)
- 2 tbsp | ¼ | ½ cup frozen peas (thawed)
- 10 | 20 | 40 g pitted green olives (quartered)
- 1 tbsp | 2 tbsp | ¼ cup continental parsley (chopped)
- ¼ | ½ | 1 tbsp lemon juice
- ¼ | ½ | 1 tbsp extra virgin olive oil
- 20 | 40 | 80 g pomegranate seeds

## Directions:

1. Set oven to 400 °F/200 °C or 360 °F/180 °C, fan forced.
2. Grease a large baking tray and line with parchment paper.
3. Spread the eggplant and cauliflower over the tray and spray lightly with oil. Dust with two-thirds of the garam masala and sesame seeds.
4. Bake for 30 minutes until golden and tender.
5. While baking, in a pot of boiling water, add the barley for 20–25 minutes until tender. Drain.
6. Heat a chargrill pan over medium-high heat.
7. Spray the lamb and asparagus with oil, then sprinkle lamb with the remaining garam masala.
8. Cook the lamb for 3–5 minutes on each side to your liking.
9. Transfer to a plate and cover loosely with foil.
10. Chargrill the asparagus, turning until caramelized and just tender.
11. Cut into 1½ in/4 cm lengths.
12. Thinly slice the lamb.

13. Combine the roasted vegetables, barley, lamb, asparagus, peas, olives, and parsley in a large bowl.
14. Add the lemon juice and oil, then toss gently. Season.
15. Sprinkle with pomegranate arils. Enjoy.

### *Zucchini and Shrimp Frittata*

Frittata is always delicious and satisfying. The pop of the peas, prawns, and pine nuts makes this dish scrumptious.

**Time:** 45 minutes

**Serving Size:** 1 | 2 | 4 servings

**Prep Time:** 15 minutes

**Cook Time:** 30 minutes

**Nutritional Facts/Info:**

Calories 225

Carbs 16.9 g

Fat 6.3 g

Protein 24.6 g

**Ingredients:**

- 2 | 4 | 8 free-range eggs
- 40 | 80 | 160 ml unsweetened almond or soy milk
- ¼ | ½ | 1 tbsp parsley (chopped)
- ½ | 1 | 2 tsp lemon juice
- ½ | 1 | 2 garlic cloves (finely chopped)
- ¼ | ½ | 1 tbsp extra virgin olive oil
- 70 | 140 | 280 g prawns (peeled, deveined)
- 1 | 2 | 3 zucchinis (shredded lengthwise with a peeler)
- 10 | 20 | 40 g fresh or frozen peas
- 5 | 10 | 20 g pine nuts
- 1¼ tbsp | 2½ tbsp | ⅓ cup low-fat ricotta

- 10 | 20 | 40 g basil leaves
- 85 |175 | 350 g wholemeal ciabatta bread (sliced)

## Directions:

1. Set oven to 400 °F/200 °C.
2. Whisk milk, eggs, and parsley in a large jug. Crack with pepper.
3. Heat the oil in a medium-size ovenproof frying pan on medium.
4. Add lemon juice and garlic, then cook for 30 seconds.
5. Add prawns, most of the zucchini, and peas to the pan. Stir for 4 minutes until prawns are almost cooked and just starting to color.
6. Pour the egg mixture into the pan and cook for 2 minutes until the frittata starts to set.
7. With a teaspoon, dot the frittata top with ricotta.
8. Place frying pan in oven and bake for 20 minutes until golden and just set.
9. Dress the frittata with pine nuts, remaining zucchini, and basil leaves.
10. Serve with ciabatta bread.

### *Anchovy and Pesto Pizzas*

Using pre-made whole grain pizza bases covered in Mediterranean vegetables makes for a quick and easy lunch or dinner.

**Time:** 20 minutes

**Serving Size:** 1 | 2 | 4 servings

**Prep Time:** 5 minutes

**Cook Time:** 15 minutes

**Nutritional Facts/Info:**

Calories 581

Carbs 71.2 g

Fat 28.4 g

Protein 38.8 g

## Ingredients:

- 1 | 2 | 4 whole grain 5 in/13 cm pizza bases
- 2 tbsp | ¼ | ½ cup passata
- 20 | 40 | 80 g basil pesto
- 30 | 60 | 120 g low-fat mozzarella (grated)
- 30 | 60 | 120 g pitted kalamata olives
- 30 | 60 | 120 g mushrooms (sliced thinly)
- ¼ | ½ | 1 large yellow capsicum (deseeded, thinly sliced)
- 35 | 75 | 150 g pancetta (torn)
- 2 | 4 | 8 anchovies (drained, chopped)
- 30 | 60 | 120 g goat's cheese (crumbled)
- Fresh basil leaves (to serve)

## Directions:

1. Set oven to 500 °F/250 °C with 2 baking trays in the oven.
2. Spread half the bases with passata and pesto over the rest.
3. Top with the mozzarella, olives, mushroom, capsicum, and goat's cheese.
4. On the passata pizza, crumble the anchovies.
5. On the pesto pizza, crumble the pancetta.
6. Bake pizzas for 10 minutes or until the bases crisp and mozzarella melts.
7. Slice with pizza cutter, top with basil, and serve.

### *Spicy Spinach and Lentil Stew*

Ready in just half an hour, this spicy stew will warm the cockles of your heart and satisfy you.

**Time:** 30 minutes

**Serving Size:** 1 | 2 | 4 servings

**Prep Time:** 10 minutes

**Cook Time:** 20 minutes

**Nutritional Facts/Info:**

Calories 265

Carbs 38.3 g

Fat 9.4 g

Protein 10.7 g

**Ingredients:**

- ½ | 1 | 2 tbsp extra virgin olive oil
- ¼ | ½ | 1 onion (diced)
- ¼ | ½ | 1 carrot (diced)
- ½ | 1 | 2 celery sticks (diced)
- 25 | 50 | 100 g sweet potato (diced)
- ¼ | ½ | 1 long red chili (deseeded, sliced finely)
- ¼ | ½ | 1 tbsp curry powder
- ¼ | ½ | 1 tbsp paprika
- ¾ | 1½ | 3 cloves garlic (crushed)
- ½ | 1 | 2 cups salt-reduced vegetable stock
- 100 | 200 | 400 g tomatoes (diced)
- 100 | 200 |400 g can lentils (rinsed, drained)
- 1 | 2 | 4 large spinach leaves (chopped with stems)
- ¼ | ½ | 1 cup green beans (tipped, chopped)
- ¼ | ½ | 1 tbsp lemon juice
- 2 tbsp | ¼ | ½ cup fresh coriander (chopped)

**Directions:**

1. Heat oil in a large deep frying pan over medium-high heat.
2. Add the diced vegetables and sauté for 5 minutes.

3. Add curry powder, paprika, garlic, and half the chili, then stir while cooking for 1 minute until fragrant.

4. Add vegetable stock, tomatoes, lentils, and beans, then bring to a boil.

5. Reduce heat to medium-low and simmer uncovered for 8 minutes until vegetables are tender.

6. Stir in spinach and lemon juice, then cook until spinach wilts. Season.

7. Transfer to serving bowls, then scatter with coriander and remaining chili. Enjoy.

### *Dukkah Salmon with Apple and Brussels Sprout Salad*

A quick and easy recipe that looks and tastes fabulous.

**Time:** 25 minutes

**Serving Size:** 1 | 2 | 4 servings

**Prep Time:** 15 minutes

**Cook Time:** 10 minutes

**Nutritional Facts/Info:**

Calories 493

Carbs 44 g

Fat 20.8 g

Protein 32.2 g

**Ingredients:**

- 1 | 2 | 4 x 115 g skinless salmon fillets
- 1 tbsp | 2 tbsp | ¼ cup extra virgin olive oil
- ½ | 1 | 2 tbsp pistachio dukkah
- ¼ | ½ | 1 cup couscous

Apple and Brussels Sprout Salad:

- 75 | 150| 300 g baby brussels sprouts (trimmed and sliced thinly)
- ¼ | ½ | 1 Pink Lady apple (sliced thinly)
- 1½ tbsp | 3 tbsp | ⅓ cup natural toasted almond kernels (roughly chopped)
- ¼ | ½ | 1 tsp sunflower seeds
- ¼ | ½ | 1 tbsp lemon juice
- ¼ | ½ | 1 lemon (cut into cheeks, to serve)

## Directions:

1. Rub the salmon with 1 tbsp olive oil.
2. Sprinkle both sides with dukkah and pat gently to secure to fish.
3. Place couscous in a bowl, add 1 cup boiling water, and stir.
4. Cover and stand for 5 minutes, then stir with a fork.
5. In the meantime, heat the remaining oil in a frying pan on medium.
6. Cook salmon for 3 minutes on each side or to your liking.
7. To make the salad, add all ingredients to a bowl, season, and toss.
8. Serve the salmon with couscous, salad, and lemon cheeks.

***Mushroom and Zucchini Risotto with Bonito Flakes***

This dish originates in Northern Italy and is a creamy, comforting dish perfect for a cold day. The bonito flakes add a little theater by waving in the steam.

**Time:** 50 minutes

**Serving Size:** 1 | 2 | 4 servings

**Prep Time:** 10 minutes

**Cook Time:** 35 minutes

**Nutritional Facts/Info:**

Calories 180

Carbs 19.7 g

Fat 8.1 g

Protein 5.1 g

**Ingredients:**

- 1⅜ | 2¾ | 5½ cups vegetable stock
- ½ | 1 | 2 tbsp extra virgin olive oil
- ½ | 1 | 2 French shallots (diced)
- ½ | 1 | 2 cloves garlic (crushed)
- 65 | 125 | 250 g mushrooms (sliced)
- ⅓ | ⅔ | 1⅓ cup arborio rice or brown rice
- 2 tbsp | ¼ | ½ cup white wine
- ¼ | ½ | 1 zucchini (sliced)
- ½ | 1 | 2 tbsp parmesan cheese (grated, plus extra to serve)
- ¼ | ½ | 1 tbsp parsley (chopped)
- ½ | 1 | 2 tbsp bonito flakes (to serve)

**Directions:**

1. Add stock to a medium saucepan and boil. Turn off.
2. In a large saucepan over medium heat, add the oil.
3. Add shallots and garlic, then sauté for a minute.

4. Add mushrooms and cook for 3 minutes.
5. Add rice and shake the pan to coat the rice.
6. Pour in wine and stir until evaporated.
7. Ladle stock into the pan, one ladle at a time, and stir gently while cooking.
8. As the stock evaporates, keep adding another ladle and continue stirring.
9. When there are only a few ladles of stock left, add the zucchinis, then continue ladling using all the stock.
10. Test the rice is al dente, then remove from heat.
11. Stir in the parmesan and ladle onto plates.
12. Bring a few mushrooms and zucchinis to the surface to dress the top.
13. Dust with extra parmesan and parsley.
14. Sprinkle with bonito flakes and serve.

### *Crumbed Aubergine with Crispy Pear Slaw*

A tasty alternative for vegans and vegetarians that regular diners will also love.

**Time:** 35 minutes

**Serving Size:** 1 | 2 | 4 servings

**Prep Time:** 15 minutes

**Cook Time:** 20 minutes

**Nutritional Facts/Info:**

Calories 324

Carbs 43.7 g

Fat 15.4 g

Protein 9.7 g

**Ingredients:**

- 1 tbsp | 2 tbsp | ¼ cup chickpea or rice flour
- 1 tbsp | 2 tbsp | ¼ cup unsweetened almond milk
- 2 tsp | ¼ | ½ cup flat leaf parsley leaves (half finely chopped)
- 25 | 50 | 100 g wholemeal panko breadcrumbs
- ¼ | ½ | 1 large eggplant (quartered lengthwise)
- Extra virgin olive oil cooking spray
- 2 tsp | ¼ | ½ red cabbage (finely shredded)
- ½ | 1 | 2 pears (halved, cored, and thinly sliced into batons)
- 11 | 22 | 45 g natural sliced almonds
- ¼ | ½ | 1 tbsp red wine vinegar
- ½ | 1 | 2 tbsp extra virgin olive oil

## Directions:

1. Set oven to 470 °F/240 °C or 430 °F/220 °C fan forced. Line a baking tray with parchment paper.
2. In a shallow bowl, mix the flour and milk together.
3. In another shallow bowl, mix the panko crumbs with parsley. Crack with pepper.
4. Dip the eggplant slices into batter allowing excess to drain.
5. Coat in crumb mixture, then place in a single layer on the tray.
6. Spray with oil and bake for 10 minutes.
7. Flip the eggplant and spray with oil again. Continue to bake for 10 minutes until golden and tender.
8. Meanwhile, mix vinegar and oil in a cup. Season with pepper.
9. In a serving bowl, mix cabbage, almonds, pear, and remaining parsley.
10. Just before serving, pour the dressing over the salad.
11. Serve the crumbed eggplant with the slaw.

# CHAPTER 7
## 4-WEEK MEAL PLAN

## TIPS FOR SUCCESSFUL MEAL PLANNING

Here are some suggestions you can consider to make meal planning quicker and easier:

- Print out the weekly meal plan of your choice and cross the meals off when eaten.
- Alternatively, utilize the blank meal plan and write your preferred meals into each day.
- Stocktake your fridge, pantry, and freezer so you know what food you already have on hand.
- Look up the recipes to see the ingredients you have on hand, what you can use to substitute, and what you need to buy.
- Write a shopping list and note the recipes you are buying ingredients for at the top of the page with a symbol next to it. Then mark the symbol next to the ingredients that are specific to that recipe. This saves using an ingredient that was meant for another meal.
- Know in advance that you can swap the meals around on

different days, depending on how you feel about cooking and availability.

- When you have time, consider making batches of food, then freezing them to use later in the week.
- Always consider using leftovers for lunch or toward another meal.
- Understand which foods to avoid, and make a conscious effort to replace those with healthy alternatives.
- When you feel peckish after dinner, consider eating a piece of fruit or having a cup of tea to fill the gap.

## Blank Meal Plan

This blank meal plan is included so you can print it out and fill it in with your own choice of meals.

| Day | Breakfast | Snack | Lunch | Snack | Dinner |
|---|---|---|---|---|---|
| Monday | | | | | |
| Tuesday | | | | | |
| Wednesday | | | | | |
| Thursday | | | | | |
| Friday | | | | | |
| Saturday | | | | | |
| Sunday | | | | | |

## THE 4-WEEK MEAL PLAN

### *Week 1*

| Day | Breakfast | Snack | Lunch | Snack | Dinner |
|---|---|---|---|---|---|
| Monday | Garlic Mushrooms with Crusty Bread | Fruity Popcorn Bar | Pesto Chicken Soup with Chickpeas | A handful of mixed seeds | Smoked Salmon, Fennel, and Avocado Salad |
| Tuesday | Summer Chia Puddings | Pepita Date Muffins | Apple and Nut Salad | Spanish Sardine Salad on Toast | Quinoa Salad with Summer Fruit |
| Wednesday | Savory Oats with Crisp Veggies | Lean Green Smoothie | Tuna Penne Salad | Roasted Chickpea Snack | Lamb and Veggie Soup with Barley |
| Thursday | Bruschetta with Cottage Cheese, Pears, and Hazelnut | A handful of nuts and seeds | Green Leek and Potato Soup with Paprika Crisps | Herbed Hummus Dip | Dukkah Salmon with Apple and Brussel Sprout Salad |
| Friday | Berry Bran Smoothie | Maple Seed Balls | Watermelon Salad with Blue Cheese | Roasted Peppers with Homemade Labneh | Chargrilled Lamb with Roasted Cauliflower and Barley |
| Saturday | Coffee Pikelets with Fruit | A handful of mixed seeds and raisins | Speedy Seafood Spaghetti | Spicy Pumpkin Hummus with Pita Crispbread | Veggie Moussaka with Tzatziki |
| Sunday | Summer Fun Smoothie Bowl | Salty Sweet Crispy Snack | Crumbed Aubergine with Crispy Pear Slaw | Pepita Date Muffins | Greek Chicken Soup with Lemon |

## *Week 2*

| Day | Breakfast | Snack | Lunch | Snack | Dinner |
|-----|-----------|-------|-------|-------|--------|
| Monday | Spanish Omelet with Lemon Arugula | A sliced tomato with ½ an avocado | Insalata Nizzarda (Pasta à la Niçoise) | Pickled Vegetables (Giardiniera) | Parsnip Soup with Olives and Prosciutto Crisps |
| Tuesday | Pick-Me-Up Smoothie | Nutty Chocolate Balls | Fish Patties with Bean and Tomato Salad | A cup of crispy veggies | Anchovy and Pesto Pizzas |
| Wednesday | Low Fat Breakfast Hash | Summer Melon Snack | Funghi and Ricotta Pappardelle | A handful of nuts and dried fruit | Watermelon Salad with Blue Cheese |
| Thursday | Vegetarian Frittata | Vegan Hazelnut Spread with Strawberries | Greek Salad with Crispy Feta | Crunchy Pumpkin Seeds | Pan-Fried Lemon Mackerel |
| Friday | Berry Bran Smoothie | Spicy Zucchini and Parsnip Chips | Zucchini and Shrimp Frittata | Crudites with Herbed Nutty Dip | Barbequed Vegetable Salad with Cashew Dressing |
| Saturday | Poached Egg with Chargrilled Asparagus and Halloumi | Roasted Chickpea Snack | Stuffed Mussels with Saffron Cream | Labneh Mezze Plate | Lemon and Ricotta Pasta with Zucchini |
| Sunday | Fluffy Berry Pancakes | A handful of nuts | Chickpea and Quinoa Burgers with Herb Yogurt | Spicy Pumpkin Hummus with Pita Crispbread | Layered Polenta with Roasted Mediterranean Vegetables |

## Week 3

| Day | Breakfast | Snack | Lunch | Snack | Dinner |
|-----|-----------|-------|-------|-------|--------|
| Monday | Fruity Date Smoothie | Crunchy Mediterranean Bites | Roast Kumara Soup with Kale, Cashews, and Feta | Spicy Sardine-Stuffed Celery | Dukkah Salmon with Apple and Brussels Sprout Salad |
| Tuesday | Salsa Bruschetta with Poached Egg | Half a cup of marinated olives and feta | Broccolini Soup with Orzo | Marinated Mushrooms | Quinoa Salad with Halloumi and Nectarines |
| Wednesday | Turmeric Quinoa with Fruit and Nuts | Choc Beet Berry Smoothie | Roast Vegetables with Garlic Mustard Anchovy Oil | A handful of nuts | Sicilian Potato and Beef Soup |
| Thursday | Crunchy Cranberry Cookies | Nutty Chickpea Crispies | Bean Soup with Parsley Oil | Nutty Date Grissino | Tomato and Saffron Pasta with Pangrattato |
| Friday | Energy Booster Smoothie | Pepita Date Muffins | Tomato Vegetable Soup with Baby Bocconcini | Half a cup of shaved parmesan cheese | Anchovy and Pesto Pizzas |
| Saturday | Chargrilled Honey Plums | Healthy Popcorn Snack | Smoked Salmon, Fennel, and Avocado Salad | A handful of seeds and raisins | Pesto Chicken Soup with Chickpeas |
| Sunday | Mango, Yogurt, and Mint Smoothie | Roasted Chickpea Snack | Roast Pumpkin Gnocchi with Crispy Sage | Prawn and Veggie Sticks | Tuna Penne Salad |

## *Week 4*

| Day | Breakfast | Snack | Lunch | Snack | Dinner |
|-----|-----------|-------|-------|-------|--------|
| Monday | Grilled Portobellos with Herby Cheese | Crunchy Pumpkin Seeds | Spicy Spinach and Lentil Stew | Kofta Balls with Lemon Tzatziki | Zesty Salad with Moroccan Cod |
| Tuesday | Smoked Salmon on English Muffins | Half a cup of chopped pickles | Roast Pumpkin Chickpea Salad | Crab Cocktail with Avocado Sauce | Aubergine Lasagne with Plant-Based Mince |
| Wednesday | Bruschetta with Cottage Cheese, Pears, and Hazelnuts | Maple Seed Balls | Creamy Pea and Feta Soup with Pistachios | Greek Toasty Appetizers | Chickpea and Quinoa Burger with Herb Yogurt |
| Thursday | Coffee Chia Puddings with 3 Fruits | Fruit and Oats Smoothie | Grilled Calamari with Radicchio | Wholemeal crispbread with hummus | Vegetarian Paella with Tofu |
| Friday | Halloumi Fritters with Corn, Broccoli, and Avocado | A handful of mixed nuts | Crumbed Aubergine with Crispy Pear Slaw | Herbed Camembert with Semi-Dried Tomatoes | Smoked Cod and Potato Soup with Peas |
| Saturday | Breakfast Banana Bread | Nutty Chocolate Balls | Mushroom and Zucchini Risotto with Bonito Flakes | Wholemeal crispbread with low-fat cottage cheese and sliced gherkins | Sicilian Beef and Potato Soup |
| Sunday | Whole Grain Egg and Asparagus Tarts | Vegan Hazelnut Spread with Strawberries | Lamb and Lentil Salad with Fried Halloumi | Crudites with Herbed Nutty Dip | Veggie Moussaka with Tzatziki |

# AFTERWORD

Now that you've reached the end of this book, the next step is to start making a positive change in your life by wholeheartedly adopting the principles of the Mediterranean diet. It's very easy to cook healthy food, and the recipes contained herein are all delicious to eat. Having undertaken the regimen myself, I can honestly say that I have lost weight effortlessly and feel healthier as a result.

You'll find meal preparation becomes more ordered and straightforward with the end results being simply delicious. Children really like to help prepare and eat, and it's a smarter way to offer attractive, healthy food to your guests when entertaining. Making good, nutritious food with love is always rewarded with compliments.

I know you and your family will benefit from changing your lifestyle to that of the Mediterraneans. By creating new habits that are beneficial to your longevity, you simply can't go wrong. You will gain enormously from what you put into it, and reap the benefits over time. But even more importantly, you can look forward to enjoying improved relationships with friends and family that join you for meals, as well as having a more realistic, outgoing, and optimistic outlook on life.

I wish you all the very best and look forward to your healthier, happier future.

*"Food can bring people together like nothing else could." –Yotam Ottolenghi*

# REFERENCES

Beunza, J.-J., Toledo, E., Hu, F. B., Bes-Rastrollo, M., Serrano-Martínez, M., Sánchez-Villegas, A., Martínez, J. A., and Martínez-González, M. A. (2010). Adherence to the Mediterranean diet, long-term weight change, and incident overweight or obesity: the Seguimiento Universidad de Navarra (SUN) cohort. *The American Journal of Clinical Nutrition*, *92*(6), 1484–1493. https://doi.org/10.3945/ajcn.2010.29764

Bonaccio, M., Di Castelnuovo, A., Bonanni, A., Costanzo, S., De Lucia, F., Pounis, G., Zito, F., Donati, M. B., de Gaetano, G., and Iacoviello, L. (2013). Adherence to a Mediterranean diet is associated with a better health-related quality of life: a possible role of high dietary antioxidant content. *BMJ Open*, *3*(8), e003003. https://doi.org/10.1136/bmjopen-2013-003003

Bremner, J. D., Moazzami, K., Wittbrodt, M. T., Nye, J. A., Lima, B. B., Gillespie, C. F., Rapaport, M. H., Pearce, B. D., Shah, A. J., and Vaccarino, V. (2020). Diet, Stress and Mental Health. *Nutrients*, *12*(8), 2428. https://doi.org/10.3390/nu12082428

Chrysohoou, C., Panagiotakos, D. B., Aggelopoulos, P., Kastorini, C.-M., Kehagia, I., Pitsavos, C., and Stefanadis, C. (2010). The Mediterranean diet contributes to the preservation of left ventricular systolic function and to the long-term favorable prognosis of patients who have had an acute coronary event. *The American Journal of Clinical Nutrition, 92*(1), 47–54. https://doi.org/10.3945/ajcn.2009.28982

De la Torre, R., Corella, D., Castañer, O., Martínez-González, M. A., Salas-Salvador, J., Vila, J., Estruch, R., Sorli, J. V., Arós, F., Fiol, M., Ros, E., Serra-Majem, L., Pintó, X., Gómez-Gracia, E., Lapetra, J., Ruiz-Canela, M., Basora, J., Asensio, E. M., Covas, M. I., and Fitó, M. (2017). Protective effect of homovanillyl alcohol on cardiovascular disease and total mortality: virgin olive oil, wine, and catechol-methylathion. *The American Journal of Clinical Nutrition, 105*(6), ajcn145813. https://doi.org/10.3945/ajcn.116.145813

Dernini, S., Berry, E., Serra-Majem, L., La Vecchia, C., Capone, R., Medina, F., Aranceta-Bartrina, J., Belahsen, R., Burlingame, B., Calabrese, G., Corella, D., Donini, L., Lairon, D., Meybeck, A., Pekcan, A., Piscopo, S., Yngve, A., and Trichopoulou, A. (2016). Med Diet 4.0: the Mediterranean diet with four sustainable benefits. *Public Health Nutrition, 20*(7), 1322–1330. https://doi.org/10.1017/s1368980016003177

*Diet Review: Mediterranean Diet.* (2018, December 12). The Nutrition Source. https://www.hsph.harvard.edu/nutritionsource/healthy-weight/diet-reviews/mediterranean-diet/

Echeverría, G., Tiboni, O., Berkowitz, L., Pinto, V., Samith, B., von Schultzendorff, A., Pedrals, N., Bitran, M., Ruini, C., Ryff, C. D., Del Rio, D., and Rigotti, A. (2020). Mediterranean Lifestyle to Promote Physical, Mental, and Environmental Health: The Case of Chile. *International Journal of Environmental Research and Public Health, 17*(22), 8482. https://doi.org/10.3390/ijerph17228482

Esposito, K., Ciotola, M., Giugliano, F., Schisano, B., Autorino, R., Iuliano, S., Vietri, M. T., Cioffi, M., De Sio, M., and Giugliano, D. (2007). Mediterranean diet improves sexual function in women with the metabolic syndrome. *International Journal of Impotence Research, 19*(5), 486–491. https://doi.org/10.1038/sj.ijir.3901555

Ferro-Luzzi, A., and Branca, F. (1995). Mediterranean diet, Italian-style: prototype of a healthy diet. *The American Journal of Clinical Nutrition*, *61*(6), 1338S1345S. https://doi.org/10.1093/ajcn/61.6.1338s

Finkelstein, E. A., Khavjou, O. A., Thompson, H., Trogdon, J. G., Pan, L., Sherry, B., and Dietz, W. (2012). Obesity and Severe Obesity Forecasts Through 2030. *American Journal of Preventive Medicine*, *42*(6), 563–570. https://doi.org/10.1016/j.amepre.2011.10.026

Fond, G., Young, A. H., Godin, O., Messiaen, M., Lançon, C., Auquier, P., and Boyer, L. (2020). Improving diet for psychiatric patients : High potential benefits and evidence for safety. *Journal of Affective Disorders*, *265*, 567–569. https://doi.org/10.1016/j.jad.2019.11.092

García-Morales, J. M., Lozada-Mellado, M., Hinojosa-Azaola, A., Llorente, L., Ogata-Medel, M., Pineda-Juárez, J. A., Alcocer-Varela, J., Cervantes-Gaytán, R., and Castillo-Martínez, L. (2020). Effect of a Dynamic Exercise Program in Combination With Mediterranean Diet on Quality of Life in Women With Rheumatoid Arthritis. *JCR: Journal of Clinical Rheumatology*, *26*(7S), S116. https://doi.org/10.1097/RHU.0000000000001064

Gardener, H., Wright, C. B., Gu, Y., Demmer, R. T., Boden-Albala, B., Elkind, M. S., Sacco, R. L., and Scarmeas, N. (2011). Mediterranean-style diet and risk of ischemic stroke, myocardial infarction, and vascular death: the Northern Manhattan Study. *The American Journal of Clinical Nutrition*, *94*(6), 1458–1464. https://doi.org/10.3945/ajcn.111.012799

Gaskins, A. J., Rovner, A. J., Mumford, S. L., Yeung, E., Browne, R. W., Trevisan, M., Perkins, N. J., Wactawski-Wende, J., and Schisterman, E. F. (2010). Adherence to a Mediterranean diet and plasma concentrations of lipid peroxidation in premenopausal women. *The American Journal of Clinical Nutrition*, *92*(6), 1461–1467. https://doi.org/10.3945/ajcn.110.000026

Gomez-Marin, B., Gomez-Delgado, F., Lopez-Moreno, J., Alcala-Diaz, J. F., Jimenez-Lucena, R., Torres-Peña, J. D., Garcia-Rios, A., Ortiz-Morales, A. M., Yubero-Serrano, E. M., del Mar Malagon, M., Lai, C.

Q., Delgado-Lista, J., Ordovas, J. M., Lopez-Miranda, J., and Perez-Martinez, P. (2018). Long-term consumption of a Mediterranean diet improves postprandial lipemia in patients with type 2 diabetes: the Cordioprev randomized trial. *The American Journal of Clinical Nutrition*, *108*(5), 963–970. https://doi.org/10.1093/ajcn/nqy144

Guasch-Ferré, M., Santos, J. L., Martínez-González, M. A., Clish, C. B., Razquin, C., Wang, D., Liang, L., Li, J., Dennis, C., Corella, D., Muñoz-Bravo, C., Romaguera, D., Estruch, R., Santos-Lozano, J. M., Castañer, O., Alonso-Gómez, A., Serra-Majem, L., Ros, E., Canudas, S., and Asensio, E. M. (2020). Glycolysis/gluconeogenesis- and tricarboxylic acid cycle–related metabolites, Mediterranean diet, and type 2 diabetes. *The American Journal of Clinical Nutrition*, *111*(4), 835–844. https://doi.org/10.1093/ajcn/nqaa016

Guasch-Ferré, M., Zheng, Y., Ruiz-Canela, M., Hruby, A., Martínez-González, M. A., Clish, C. B., Corella, D., Estruch, R., Ros, E., Fitó, M., Dennis, C., Morales-Gil, I. M., Arós, F., Fiol, M., Lapetra, J., Serra-Majem, L., Hu, F. B., and Salas-Salvadó, J. (2016). Plasma acylcarnitines and risk of cardiovascular disease: effect of Mediterranean diet interventions. *The American Journal of Clinical Nutrition*, *103*(6), 1408–1416. https://doi.org/10.3945/ajcn.116.130492

Helsing, E. (1995). Traditional diets and disease patterns of the Mediterranean, circa 1960. *The American Journal of Clinical Nutrition*, *61*(6), 1329S1337S. https://doi.org/10.1093/ajcn/61.6.1329s

Jennings, A., Cashman, K. D., Gillings, R., Cassidy, A., Tang, J., Fraser, W., Dowling, K. G., Hull, G. L. J., Berendsen, A. A. M., de Groot, L. C. P. G. M., Pietruszka, B., Wierzbicka, E., Ostan, R., Bazzocchi, A., Battista, G., Caumon, E., Meunier, N., Malpuech-Brugère, C., Franceschi, C., and Santoro, A. (2018). A Mediterranean-like dietary pattern with vitamin D3 (10 µg/d) supplements reduced the rate of bone loss in older Europeans with osteoporosis at baseline: results of a 1-y randomized controlled trial. *The American Journal of Clinical Nutrition*, *108*(3), 633–640. https://doi.org/10.1093/ajcn/nqy122

Jospe, M. R., Roy, M., Brown, R. C., Haszard, J. J., Meredith-Jones, K., Fangupo, L. J., Osborne, H., Fleming, E. A., and Taylor, R. W. (2019).

Intermittent fasting, Paleolithic, or Mediterranean diets in the real world: exploratory secondary analyses of a weight-loss trial that included choice of diet and exercise. *The American Journal of Clinical Nutrition*, *111*(3), 503–514. https://doi.org/10.1093/ajcn/nqz330

Karstens, A. J., Tussing-Humphreys, L., Zhan, L., Rajendran, N., Cohen, J., Dion, C., Zhou, X. J., and Lamar, M. (2019). Associations of the Mediterranean diet with cognitive and neuroimaging phenotypes of dementia in healthy older adults. *The American Journal of Clinical Nutrition*, *109*(2), 361–368. https://doi.org/10.1093/ajcn/nqy275

Lopez-Garcia, E., Hagan, K. A., Fung, T. T., Hu, F. B., and Rodríguez-Artalejo, F. (2018). Mediterranean diet and risk of frailty syndrome among women with type 2 diabetes. *The American Journal of Clinical Nutrition*, *107*(5), 763–771. https://doi.org/10.1093/ajcn/nqy026

Lopez-Garcia, E., Rodriguez-Artalejo, F., Li, T. Y., Fung, T. T., Li, S., Willett, W. C., Rimm, E. B., and Hu, F. B. (2013). The Mediterranean-style dietary pattern and mortality among men and women with cardiovascular disease. *The American Journal of Clinical Nutrition*, *99*(1), 172–180. https://doi.org/10.3945/ajcn.113.068106

López-Olivares, M., Mohatar-Barba, M., Fernández-Gómez, E., and Enrique-Mirón, C. (2020). Mediterranean Diet and the Emotional Well-Being of Students of the Campus of Melilla (University of Granada). *Nutrients*, *12*(6), 1826. https://doi.org/10.3390/nu12061826

Mahamat-Saleh, Y., Cervenka, I., Al Rahmoun, M., Savoye, I., Mancini, F. R., Trichopoulou, A., Boutron-Ruault, M.-C., and Kvaskoff, M. (2019). Mediterranean dietary pattern and skin cancer risk: A prospective cohort study in French women. *The American Journal of Clinical Nutrition*, *110*(4), 993–1002. https://doi.org/10.1093/ajcn/nqz173

Marcus, M., Yasami, M. T., van Ommeren, M., Chisjolm, D., and Saxena, S. (2012). *DEPRESSION: A Global Crisis*. https://www.who.int/mental_health/management/depression/wfmh_paper_depression_wmhd_2012.pdf

Martinez-Lacoba, R., Pardo-Garcia, I., Amo-Saus, E., and Escribano-Sotos, F. (2018). Mediterranean diet and health outcomes: a systematic meta-review. *European Journal of Public Health*, *28*(5), 955–961. https://doi.org/10.1093/eurpub/cky113

Mena, M.-P., Sacanella, E., Vazquez-Agell, M., Morales, M., Fitó, M., Escoda, R., Serrano-Martínez, M., Salas-Salvadó, J., Benages, N., Casas, R., Lamuela-Raventós, R. M., Masanes, F., Ros, E., and Estruch, R. (2008). Inhibition of circulating immune cell activation: a molecular antiinflammatory effect of the Mediterranean diet. *The American Journal of Clinical Nutrition*, *89*(1), 248–256. https://doi.org/10.3945/ajcn.2008.26094

Merle, B. M., Silver, R. E., Rosner, B., and Seddon, J. M. (2015). Adherence to a Mediterranean diet, genetic susceptibility, and progression to advanced macular degeneration: a prospective cohort study. *The American Journal of Clinical Nutrition*, *102*(5), 1196–1206. https://doi.org/10.3945/ajcn.115.111047

Moravejolahkami, A. R., Paknahad, Z., Chitsaz, A., Hojjati Kermani, M. A., and Borzoo-Isfahani, M. (2020). Potential of modified Mediterranean diet to improve quality of life and fatigue severity in multiple sclerosis patients: a single-center randomized controlled trial. *International Journal of Food Properties*, *23*(1), 1993–2004. https://doi.org/10.1080/10942912.2020.1840390

Muñoz, M.-A., Fíto, M., Marrugat, J., Covas, M.-I., and Schröder, H. (2008). Adherence to the Mediterranean diet is associated with better mental and physical health. *British Journal of Nutrition*, *101*(12), 1821–1827. https://doi.org/10.1017/S0007114508143598

Muralidharan, J., Moreno-Indias, I., Bulló, M., Lopez, J. V., Corella, D., Castañer, O., Vidal, J., Atzeni, A., Fernandez-García, J. C., Torres-Collado, L., Fernández-Carrión, R., Fito, M., Olbeyra, R., Gomez-Perez, A. M., Galiè, S., Bernal-López, M. R., Martinez-Gonzalez, M. A., Salas-Salvadó, J., and Tinahones, F. J. (2021). Effect on gut microbiota of a 1-y lifestyle intervention with Mediterranean diet compared with energy-reduced Mediterranean diet and physical activity promotion: PREDIMED-Plus Study. *The American Journal of Clinical Nutrition*. https://doi.org/10.1093/ajcn/nqab150

Nestle, M. (1995). Mediterranean diets: historical and research overview. *The American Journal of Clinical Nutrition*, *61*(6), 1313S1320S. https://doi.org/10.1093/ajcn/61.6.1313s

Parletta, N., Zarnowiecki, D., Cho, J., Wilson, A., Bogomolova, S., Villani, A., Itsiopoulos, C., Niyonsenga, T., Blunden, S., Meyer, B., Segal, L., Baune, B. T., and O'Dea, K. (2017). A Mediterranean-style dietary intervention supplemented with fish oil improves diet quality and mental health in people with depression: A randomized controlled trial (HELFIMED). *Nutritional Neuroscience*, *22*(7), 474–487. https://doi.org/10.1080/1028415x.2017.1411320

Rodriguez, A., Curhan, G. C., Gambaro, G., Taylor, E. N., and Ferraro, P. M. (2020). Mediterranean diet adherence and risk of incident kidney stones. *The American Journal of Clinical Nutrition*, *111*(5). https://doi.org/10.1093/ajcn/nqaa066

Romaguera, D., Norat, T., Vergnaud, A.-C., Mouw, T., May, A. M., Agudo, A., Buckland, G., Slimani, N., Rinaldi, S., Couto, E., Clavel-Chapelon, F., Boutron-Ruault, M.-C., Cottet, V., Rohrmann, S., Teucher, B., Bergmann, M., Boeing, H., Tjønneland, A., Halkjaer, J., and Jakobsen, M. U. (2010). Mediterranean dietary patterns and prospective weight change in participants of the EPIC-PANACEA project. *The American Journal of Clinical Nutrition*, *92*(4), 912–921. https://doi.org/10.3945/ajcn.2010.29482

Ruini, L. F., Ciati, R., Pratesi, C. A., Marino, M., Principato, L., and Vannuzzi, E. (2015). Working toward Healthy and Sustainable Diets: The "Double Pyramid Model" Developed by the Barilla Center for Food and Nutrition to Raise Awareness about the Environmental and Nutritional Impact of Foods. *Frontiers in Nutrition*, *2*. https://doi.org/10.3389/fnut.2015.00009

Sánchez-Villegas, A., Delgado-Rodríguez, M., Alonso, A., Schlatter, J., Lahortiga, F., Majem, L. S., and Martínez-González, M. A. (2009). Association of the Mediterranean Dietary Pattern With the Incidence of Depression. *Archives of General Psychiatry*, *66*(10), 1090. https://doi.org/10.1001/archgenpsychiatry.2009.129

Shannon, O. M., Stephan, B. C. M., Granic, A., Lentjes, M., Hayat, S., Mulligan, A., Brayne, C., Khaw, K.-T., Bundy, R., Aldred, S., Hornberger, M., Paddick, S.-M., Muniz-Tererra, G., Minihane, A.-M., Mathers, J. C., and Siervo, M. (2019). Mediterranean diet adherence and cognitive function in older UK adults: the European Prospective Investigation into Cancer and Nutrition–Norfolk (EPIC-Norfolk) Study. *The American Journal of Clinical Nutrition*, *110*(4), 938–948. https://doi.org/10.1093/ajcn/nqz114

Sofi, F., Abbate, R., Gensini, G. F., and Casini, A. (2010). Accruing evidence on benefits of adherence to the Mediterranean diet on health: an updated systematic review and meta-analysis. *The American Journal of Clinical Nutrition*, *92*(5), 1189–1196. https://doi.org/10.3945/ajcn.2010.29673

Strujik, E. A., Hagan, K. A., Fung, T. T., Hu, F. B., Rodríguez-Artalejo, F., and Lopez-Garcia, E. (2020). Diet quality and risk of frailty among older women in the Nurses' Health Study. *The American Journal of Clinical Nutrition*, *111*(4), 877–883. https://doi.org/10.1093/ajcn/nqaa028

Trichopoulou, A., Bamia, C., Lagiou, P., and Trichopoulos, D. (2010). Conformity to traditional Mediterranean diet and breast cancer risk in the Greek EPIC (European Prospective Investigation into Cancer and Nutrition) cohort. *The American Journal of Clinical Nutrition*, *92*(3), 620–625. https://doi.org/10.3945/ajcn.2010.29619

Tsaban, G., Wolak, A., Avni-Hassid, H., Gepner, Y., Shelef, I., Henkin, Y., Schwarzfuchs, D., Cohen, N., Bril, N., Rein, M., Serfaty, D., Kenigsbuch, S., Tene, L., Zelicha, H., Yaskolka-Meir, A., Komy, O., Bilitzky, A., Chassidim, Y., Ceglarek, U., and Stumvoll, M. (2017). Dynamics of intrapericardial and extrapericardial fat tissues during long-term, dietary-induced, moderate weight loss. *The American Journal of Clinical Nutrition*, *106*(4), 984–995. https://doi.org/10.3945/ajcn.117.157115

*UNESCO - Mediterranean diet.* (2019). Unesco.org. https://ich.unesco.org/en/RL/mediterranean-diet-00884

Ventriglio, A., Sancassiani, F., Contu, M. P., Latorre, M., Di Slavatore, M., Fornaro, M., and Bhugra, D. (2020). Mediterranean Diet and its

Benefits on Health and Mental Health: A Literature Review. *Clinical Practice and Epidemiology in Mental Health : CP and EMH*, *16*(Suppl-1), 156–164. https://doi.org/10.2174/1745017902016010156

Wade, A. T., Davis, C. R., Dyer, K. A., Hodgson, J. M., Woodman, R. J., and Murphy, K. (2018). A Mediterranean diet supplemented with dairy foods improves markers of cardiovascular risk: results from the MedDairy randomized controlled trial. *The American Journal of Clinical Nutrition*, *108*(6), 1166–1182. https://doi.org/10.1093/ajcn/nqy207

Wengreen, H., Munger, R. G., Cutler, A., Quach, A., Bowles, A., Corcoran, C., Tschanz, J. T., Norton, M. C., and Welsh-Bohmer, K. A. (2013). Prospective study of Dietary Approaches to Stop Hypertension– and Mediterranean-style dietary patterns and age-related cognitive change: the Cache County Study on Memory, Health and Aging. *The American Journal of Clinical Nutrition*, *98*(5), 1263–1271. https://doi.org/10.3945/ajcn.112.051276

World Health Organisation. (2020, September 21). *Dementia*. Who.int; World Health Organization: WHO. https://www.who.int/news-room/fact-sheets/detail/dementia

Wu, J., Song, X., Chen, G.-C., Neelakantan, N., van Dam, R. M., Feng, L., Yuan, J.-M., Pan, A., and Koh, W.-P. (2019). Dietary pattern in midlife and cognitive impairment in late life: a prospective study in Chinese adults. *The American Journal of Clinical Nutrition*, *110*(4), 912–920. https://doi.org/10.1093/ajcn/nqz150

Yotam, O. (n.d.). *Yotam Ottolenghi Quotes*. BrainyQuote. Retrieved September 4, 2021, from https://www.brainyquote.com/quotes/yotam_ottolenghi_606434

IMAGES

Doan, Trang. "Photo of Assorted Sliced Fruits in White Ceramic Bowl." *Pexels.com*, www.pexels.com/photo/assorted-sliced-fruits-in-white-ceramic-bowl-1092730/.

---. "Photo of Bread with Fruits." *Pexels.com*, www.pexels.com/photo/photo-of-bread-with-fruits-981034/.

Elliott, Taryn. "Photo of Red and White Fruits on Wooden Board." *Pexels.com*, www.pexels.com/photo/red-and-white-round-fruits-on-brown-wooden-bowl-4099237/.

Fauxels. "Photo of People Sharing Food." *Pexels.com*, www.pexels.com/photo/sharing-cherry-tomatoes-3184188/.

Foto-Rabe. "Photo of Mediterranean Vegetables and Herbs." *Pixabay.com*, pixabay.com/photos/vegetables-mediterranean-herbs-1201413/.

Lisa. "Photo of Pasta with Tomato and Basil." *Pexels.com*, www.pexels.com/photo/selective-focus-photography-of-pasta-with-tomato-and-basil-1279330/.

"Mediterranean Diet Pyramid: A Lifestyle for Today." *Predimed*, 2010, www.predimed.es/pyramids.html.

Michalou, Nicole. "Photo of Person Pouring Wine at Dinner Table." *Pexels.com*, www.pexels.com/photo/person-pouring-wine-on-glass-5775055/.

Ra, Navada. "Photo of Bowl of Soup and Two Silver Spoons." *Pexels.com*, www.pexels.com/photo/bowl-of-soup-and-two-silver-spoons-1703272/.

Shaislionfish. "Photo of Fresh Appetizer Meals." *Pixabay.com*, pixabay.com/photos/appetizers-salad-food-meal-fresh-2222361/.

Printed in Great Britain
by Amazon